D1431021

UnCommon Preaching

UnCommon Preaching

An Alternative to the Lectionary

SUSAN E. CARTMELL

WIPF & STOCK · Eugene, Oregon

UNCOMMON PREACHING
An Alternative to the Lectionary

Wipf & Stock
An Imprint of Wipf and Stock Publishers
199 W. 8th Ave., Suite 3
Eugene, OR 97401

www.wipfandstock.com

ISBN 13: 978-1-4982-0445-3

Manufactured in the U .S.A.

Contents

Acknowledgments

THROUGHOUT THE PROCESS OF writing this book, I owe a lot to the encouragement of others. First and foremost, I feel indebted to the people in the churches I have served, especially the people in The Congregational Church of Needham, where I currently serve as Senior Minister. Though many people see preaching as a form of oratory, it also has the potential to become more like an open conversation, and even a dialogue. Each week the people of the Congregational Church of Needham have given me the gift of their attention. From the time I arrived I could see it in their eyes when I spoke. I could feel the curiosity and openness and I did not want to disappoint them, but it was more than that. Each week I really wanted to reach them and share my best ideas about faith with them. The relationship that emerged between pulpit and pew propelled us all on a journey of discovery. Together we found a new way to worship. This book is the story of that journey.

I am also indebted to the faculty and students at Andover Newton Theological School. As our church developed a different way to organize worship, I recognized that I was charting new territory. Designing worship outside the framework of the *New Revised Common Lectionary* felt, at first, like steering a ship into uncharted waters without a compass. So, I enrolled in the Doctor of Ministry Program at Andover Newton to find some reference points and verify that I was not taking us too far afield. This book is both a report on what we have learned in my own church, and an examination of the history of worship that gave me the confidence to believe we were on reliable, theological footing. I have come to see that this experience has been a wonderful example of the authentic connection between the scholarship of the academy and the practice of ministry. It has taught me how the questions of practical church leadership can promote further academic pursuits, and how new scholarship can enrich and revitalize parish work and life.

Many conversations in church meetings and hallways convinced me that folks were interested in this project, and wanted me to see it through. I am very grateful to the Deacons of the Needham Church for the way they encouraged my creativity with their openness to new ideas about worship, their enthusiasm for change, their trust in my judgment, and their feedback that was both supportive and discerning. Time and again their generous comments buoyed me and reminded me that we were in this enterprise together. I am also indebted to the people I interviewed. Mary Luti talked openly about Christian liturgy and helped me to see the significance of the Christian calendar throughout the history of the church; that clear distinction affected my thinking throughout this project. I was also very touched by the hospitality of Horace Allen. He invited me to his home to talk candidly and brilliantly about worship; it would be hard to thank him adequately. Greg Mobley's practical advice, Biblical integrity, and sense of humor were a source of encouragement. From the first time she heard about this project, Beth Nordbeck has believed in it and championed it in ways that fortified my resolve to see it through; I am very grateful for her guidance and advice.

Finally, for years now, I have found inspiration from my children and their spouses: Jonathan and Nancy, Elizabeth and Seth, and Sarah and Paul. In particular, Jonathan's feedback and editing ideas proved enormously helpful. And of course, my wife, Peggy O'Connor, has been my true partner in every way throughout this journey.

Introduction

The Church's Current Challenge

I WROTE THIS BOOK to tell you about my journey as a preacher and pastor. I started on this path because I was convinced that people come to worship with the purpose of searching for meaning in their lives. Whether they articulate it or not, they come seeking an alternative to our contemporary secular values. They come searching for inspiration to deal with personal concerns that have tied them up in knots, and often they don't know where else to go for insights or peace of mind. I believe that, though few will ask for it, most people also come searching for instruction in faith, and a different perspective about life that will fill their spiritual hunger. The good news here is that they come seeking exactly what most churches have to offer, but the bad news is that too often we don't deliver our message in a way that works. At least in our church there was a real dis-connect. Our use of the lectionary did not serve us well; it did not prove to be the best way to communicate the life-giving messages of faith that people were searching for. So we changed the way we do worship. It is my hope that this book may spark a conversation in other churches, and perhaps it will touch a place in the hearts and minds of other pastors who are seeking to address the spiritual hunger they see in their people today.

Since biblical times, whenever people have gathered for worship, the cornerstone of that experience has been some form of address that connected God's story to the lives of the faithful. Based on readings from sacred scripture, these oral presentations have taught people about faith and inspired them to find a deeper purpose for life every week. This tradition of delivering sermons has been practiced in Judaism and Christianity for at least twenty-five centuries, and though preaching has a time-honored place in the history of worship, over the course of time this tradition has benefitted from reforms in style and scope. Periods of societal reform have often gone hand in hand with changes in worship. One might argue that a source of strength in the preaching tradition comes from the church's ability to allow worship patterns to change enough to make the overall tradition sustainable.

As a Protestant pastor in a suburban church outside of Boston, I have been a long-time student of preaching. As the senior minister I lead worship and oversee a program of sermon topics for the church year. For many years, preaching has been the central focus of my work. Because of this, I have a natural curiosity about the trends in preaching, and a sense of responsibility that the messages from our pulpit be consistently engaging, instructive, and inspiring.

Over the course of my tenure in this position, I have had the opportunity to make some significant changes in the worship services, and particularly in the way we plan and deliver the sermons. This book is a report about the experience that we have had at The Congregational Church of Needham, and our journey as a community of faith as we have experimented with new preaching styles and transformed the way that we organize our worship services.

Specifically, the changes we have made involve a transition from using the *New Revised Common Lectionary* as our guide for sermon texts to developing a thematic approach to selecting preaching texts. This transition energized our services and the church program. In the process it pushed us to reconsider how we organize worship and how we envision Christian Education. We made these changes because it became clear to me that our sermons were not sufficiently effective in addressing contemporary audiences and teaching the people in our pews about our faith. We were squandering our opportunity each week to reach both new-comers and seasoned members, and so we reexamined the style and content of the sermons and embarked on an odyssey. Like all significant journeys, it has brought with it times of investigation and experimentation, as well as times of confusion and failure. In this book I will strive to explain why we made the changes we did, and why I have come to believe that they were necessary, even essential.

In the first chapter I demonstrate that worship, like every-thing else in life, has always been adapting and evolving in order to stay relevant to the changes in society and in congregations over time. Though we imagine that worship traditions have sailed above the sea of change that marks so much of history, a closer look at church history shows quite the opposite. Scanning some significant moments in the history of preaching over the last two thousand years, I take a special interest in those times of transition where change was inevitable.

In the second chapter, I explain why this is the moment when Protestant churches need to re-think some standard preaching practices and consider alternatives to the *New Revised Common Lectionary* as the primary tool for planning weekly worship. Tak-ing a broad look at cultural data, I explain why this time is ripe for innovation. I also describe my own restlessness as a worship leader and how I embarked on my own journey. My excursion took place both figuratively and literally. It involved an academic investiga-tion into alternative ways to organize worship that caused me to question my preaching style, and it also pushed me to visit other churches with robust worship around the country. I talk about what I learned and what I saw in these other churches. Finally, I recount a telling experience I had with some young adults at a Boston coffee shop, and how that experience affected my sense of the importance of this moment in the Church's history.

In chapter 3, I look closely at the *New Revised Common Lectionary* and examine some of its assumptions. Though every pattern for worship includes its own bias, often it is hard to see these assumptions until you step back and search for them. Since the 1970s, many Protestant churches have used the lectionary to guide and organize worship; so I look at the theological message at the heart of the lectionary. I also explain the shortcomings I see in the way that the lectionary uses scripture and ask whether this theology serves modern congregations as well as we think it does.

In chapter 4, I describe the way that my view of my role as a preacher has evolved. More and more I have become convinced that pastors have an important teaching role in the pulpit, which may be easily overlooked or underestimated. Using anecdotes from my church, I explain why I believe that people come to church hoping to *learn* about faith every bit as much as they hope to be inspired about it. The sermon has the potential to be their "lesson" on life and faithful living. Drawing on my experience as a pastor, I demonstrate the way that sermons offer opportunities for instruction and then I suggest some teaching goals. Finally, I introduce a set of scripture readings that I propose constitute a pulpit curriculum. I suggest that these Bible stories form a set of lesson plans that can guide and shape sermon content.

The fifth chapter demonstrates a new way to identify preaching texts by looking at scripture with an eye for biblical themes. I understand that if preachers have grown accustomed to using the lectionary to organize worship, then it requires a certain adjustment if you decide to switch to preaching with themes. In the lectionary-based system, preachers are assigned a scripture reading; in the themed-based method of preaching, they have to find a sermon text to illustrate the theme they have chosen. It transforms the way you prepare sermons and engage with scripture. That shift may even require a new way to view the Bible itself. So, in this chapter, I demonstrate how to approach the Bible with an eye toward finding topics and themes that span both testaments. I don't seek to establish the *definitive* themes in scripture here, but I *do* try to illustrate a new way to look at scripture with an eye toward overarching patterns. Hopefully, this will point toward a more holistic view of the Bible that will be helpful in identifying themes and finding ideas for how to use them in sermons.

Finally, in chapter 6, I introduce a three-year cycle for preaching with themes so that pastors and churches can consider how to use this resource. I introduce the Pulpit Curriculum, explain its significance, and then demonstrate how to coordinate a set of preaching themes with the texts in the Pulpit Curriculum. I explain how the schedule of topics has evolved in our congregation and what the scheduling considerations have been. This section concludes with a description of some of our missteps and outright failures, so that other congregations can learn from our mistakes. It is my hope that this candid look at both our successes and ongoing challenges in developing a different approach to worship will be helpful to everyone when considering the best approach to find fresh ways to deliver sermons in their own pulpits.

1

Evolving Patterns of Worship

LIKE EVERYTHING ELSE IN our lives, worship has evolved. Throughout church history, worship patterns have changed and adjusted to practical concerns as well as sacred considerations. Though worship traditions appear to be well established, they are by no means static, and never have been. If anything has been constant in the history of worship, it has been the trend of continuous adaptation. When times changed and the needs of the people did too, there is plenty of evidence that worship patterns responded to social movements, current events, and historical transitions. Patterns of worship were created to meet the needs of the churches they served. Things that people of faith have taken for granted, and assumed were immutable, were all created somewhere. They each emerged in a particular place and time as someone's best idea for that moment, and started as inventions of worshipping congregations within Jewish, Roman Catholic, and Protestant congregations. Undoubtedly, time has lent weight to these traditions and they have come to shape the faith they were originally designed to explain, but understanding their origins will make it easier to decipher which traditions make sense today and which are no longer relevant.

Today's patterns of worship among Jews and Christians have their foundation in ancient Judaism as it was practiced in the synagogues of Israel and the Temple in Jerusalem. At the center of Jewish worship were the readings from the Torah and the address by the rabbi that explained the meaning of scripture and its relevance for the lives of the people. That address was the sermon.

As early as the fifth and sixth centuries before the Christian era (BCE), Jewish rabbis used a set of readings assigned for each Sabbath. Typically, the Torah reading was followed by a Psalm or selection from the Prophets. Once the lessons were read, the rabbi would preach on them and often the congregation would discuss his exegesis and ask questions. The practice of reading assigned scripture was well established in synagogues by the time Jesus was born. Indeed, Luke's Gospel alludes to this practice in the story about Jesus' return to his home synagogue. When Jesus stood up to read, the scroll of the prophet Isaiah was handed to him (Luke 4:16–18).[1] Jesus had been handed the lectionary reading for the day, and he proceeded to read it and expand on it.

As early as 50–70 in the Christian era (CE), disciples of Jesus of Nazareth read the Hebrew Scripture passages assigned to the synagogue cycle, and then developed the habit of adding the writings of the Apostles, which were organized into supplementary cycles. Paul writes in Timothy, "Until I arrive, give attention to the "selected readings of the day."[2] In 1 Thessalonians and Colossians, Paul instructs the churches to read his letters as though they were part of the cycle of readings.[3] When the Gospels began to circulate, portions of Matthew, Mark, Luke and later John's writings were added to the worship readings.

Some scholars believe that the gospels themselves were written as a series of worship readings, or lections. In his study of the discrepancies in the synoptic gospels, Mark, Matthew and Luke, John Shelby Spong believes the synoptics were originally used in the earliest Christian communities as a series of readings that tell

1. Ring, "Path," 2.
2. Ibid.
3. Ibid.

Jesus' story in ways that corresponded to the Jewish calendar. If he is correct, the gospels represent their own lectionary—a set of worship readings for Christian worship in Jewish synagogues of the first and second centuries.[4] The stories of his life were written in a sequence that portrays Jesus as the fulfillment of the Prophets and the Law—the culmination of messianic longing and expectation. Thus, these stories about Jesus gave new meaning to the traditional Jewish holy days.

Robin Meyers supports Spong's theory and points to some details in the crucifixion story, which make it read like liturgy, not history. When they tell of Jesus carrying his own cross, and the three-hour ordeal at the center of a three-day drama, they recall the way that Abraham began to sacrifice his son Isaac by making the boy carry the wood for the fire, as they embarked on their own three-day journey. Jewish listeners would see these connections.[5] Given the implications of this scholarship, it reminds us of the ways worship may have played a central role in shaping both the theology and the history of our faith.

The Development of the Christian Calendar

Though rooted in Judaism, Christian worship took on a new character even as it maintained its Jewish ties. We recognize this in the pattern of synergy that brought so many elements together in the creation of the Christian calendar. You see evidence of the way that the early Christians found parts of the calendar in ancient traditions while other parts give evidence of a more modern heritage. When Christians set the dates to remember early Christian martyrs and the birth of Jesus, they used the Roman solar calendar, so that Christmas and the saints' days are fixed even today. But, for early Christians, Easter became the lens through which people of faith came to see the meaning of the life of Jesus. The significance of the Festival of the Resurrection would be hard to underestimate,

4. Spong, *Jesus for the Non-Religious,* 204.
5. Meyers, *Saving Jesus,* 60.

and that date changed according to the ancient lunar rhythms. When Easter was established before or around 150 CE, the date was determined by a time-honored calculation to arrive at a date on the lunar calendar used in Judaism. The most significant date in the new Christian calendar retains, even today, this ancient habit of change.

Once the celebration of Easter became established, other periods of devotion arose around it. Before long, people were fasting from Good Friday until Easter morning. By the third century, communicants preparing to join the church on the Saturday before Easter fasted for six days in preparation for the sacrament of baptism. All of the faithful anticipated the communion on Easter by observing a time of preparation that eventually lasted forty days, and corresponded to Jesus' time in the wilderness. (Sundays were never counted as times of fasting because they were always feast days and a respite during Lent.)

It is interesting to note that the word used for this season of preparation is Lent, which comes from the Germanic root meaning "spring," and Easter is named for the Anglo-Saxon goddess of spring. These European linguistic connections show that the Christian calendar emerged with a distinct prejudice for the northern hemisphere, where Lent and Easter take place in the spring, and they further demonstrate that this faith tradition emerged and was honed in a specific time and place. It follows that the worship symbols and meanings attached to them grew in a context where people connected their faith to practical considerations.

Though it might seem strange today, historically Epiphany was older and much more significant than Christmas in the formational decades of Christianity. It was not until 300 AD, however, that Epiphany was associated with the Wise Men, and it was at least fifty years later before Christmas was routinely observed in Christian communities.[6] There have always been two different dates for Christmas—January 6 and December 25. January 6 was selected as the date of Christ's baptism; immediately after his baptism Luke makes reference to the fact that Jesus is thirty

6. Calkins, *Christian Year*, 5.

years old (Luke 3:23), and so people assumed he was baptized on his birthday. A different set of assumptions lies behind the date December 25. People believed that, in John's gospel, when he says, "In the beginning was the Word and the Word was with God and the Word was God" (John 1:1), he refers to the date the world was created, which was thought to be March 25, the Vernal Equinox on the Roman calendar. Being the new creation, it was reasoned, Jesus must have been conceived on March 25; add nine months to that date and you arrive at December 25 to find the date of his birth. I mention these details to demonstrate the way that major decisions about Christian tradition have often relied on sets of assumptions that we might question or see as somewhat arbitrary today. My purpose here is not to undermine this tradition, but to illustrate the very human considerations at the heart of it.

THE SABBATH AND THE LORD'S DAY

During the formative years of the early Christian Church, the day for worship was also changing. In churches where many members came from a Jewish background, they were accustomed to worshipping on Saturday, which had always been their Sabbath. But by the time of the Council of Nicaea in 325 CE, Christians had established that Easter was on Sunday. But as Easter assumed prominence as the North Star around which the whole faith and the Christian calendar were oriented, believers were forced to rethink their day of worship. Between the second and fourth centuries CE, some communities observed the Sabbath, others transitioned to Sunday, and some observed both days. In ancient times laborers were only allowed one day of rest, and so for many years it was common to observe a Sabbath day of rest, then return to work on the first day of the week. Sunday began to be known as the "Day of God's Kingdom"—a day to work during daylight and then rejoice with a Eucharist or Thanksgiving meal at dusk. After dinner on Sundays, Christians would eat a special meal and then the people told stories about Jesus' post-resurrection appearances, and read from the book of Acts. The habit emerged of sharing the bread and cup as they told these stories, and so the practice of communion became a standard part of an evolving worship pattern. One can assume that this changed eventually in the late third century and early fourth century as fewer Christians shared a Jewish background and Gentile converts emerged as the majority. Once this happened, there was little opposition to establishing Sunday as the *one* day of rest.

Worship historian Horace Allen sees the transition from the Sabbath on Saturday to the Lord's Day on Sunday as a significant statement. The notion of the Sabbath emerged from the story of Creation as a time of rest; God worked for six days to create the world and all that was in it, but God rested on the seventh day, known as the Sabbath (Gen 2:2). But the Lord's Day is the first day of the week. It is not a time to let down after hard labor, but a time to feast with God at Christ's table. For Christians, moving worship to Sunday signified a new understanding that the remainder of the week was lived in light of the commemoration of the resurrection.[7] Now, the tone of celebration permeated a Christian's life and the life of the community. Everything that Christians did throughout the week took place in the light of the Eucharist, or Thanksgiving Feast of the Resurrection, which began the week.

The Lectionary

At the heart of the Christian calendar, and the worship liturgy that supported it, was the six-month journey beginning in Advent and culminating in Pentecost, when Christians re-enacted the life of Jesus. Remembering Jesus' birth, life, death and resurrection with seasons devoted to that story, such as Advent, Christmas, Epiphany, Lent, and Easter, worshippers accompanied their Lord through periods of penitence and celebration. The festivals of Christmas, Easter, and Pentecost served as sacred markers and high points along this path of devotion. Once the church had arrived at Pentecost, then the remaining six months was regarded as ordinary

---

7. Interview: Horace Allen.

time—as opposed to sacred time—and the scripture readings were more varied.

By the sixth century, lectionaries with lists of readings for each Sunday's worship service, and other holy days in the calendar, were widely available throughout Christendom. Many had an Old Testament passage, a gospel reading, and a portion of Paul's writings listed for each worship service.[8] However, they were not all standard: France, Spain, and Milan all had different readings for various Sundays. Priests were uniformly expected to explain the day's readings—a requirement that fostered the flourishing of preaching in the Middle Ages. As preaching grew more popular, it had an impact on church architecture in Europe. Larger churches were built and pews were added, for the first time, to accommodate the crowds who came to listen to the longer sermons. In the twelfth century, inspirational sermons became the chief way to promote the Crusades. "The fact that so many sermons have survived, written by such men as Bernard of Clairvaux, John Wycliffe, and Girolamo Savonarola, further demonstrates how highly preaching was valued at that time in history."[9]

From the earliest Christian communities, people associated special days with the life or death of various apostles, saints, or martyrs. Some martyrs garnered local respect, while others like Stephen and Paul earned wider devotion. By the Middle Ages the saints' days were enjoyed throughout Europe. Medieval market days began to coincide with religious holidays, and commercial festivals were scheduled in conjunction with the worship services on these celebrations for various saints.

Religious holy days went hand in hand with secular holidays, as the etymology indicates, and became part of the calendar until the sixteenth century, when the Protestant reformers eliminated all of the saints' days. The European reformers revised the way the Christian holy days were observed by reducing festivity in the Christian calendar. However, the original Protestant reformers never abandoned the Christian calendar entirely.

8. White, *Brief History*, 99.

9. Ibid.

The Roman Catholic Church has consistently used the lectionary readings as the backbone for the mass, but within that structure many parishes experimented with other readings too. Clergy chose from a variety of sources including the Old Testament, the Gospels, the letters of Paul, the *Lives of the Saints*, and other theological sources. With so many choices, Roman Catholics often emphasized the Gospels at the expense of Hebrew scripture, but early sixteenth century reformer, John Calvin, sought to reform the lectionary by restoring Hebrew scripture to a prominence unknown for many generations. The Swiss reformer, Calvin, distinguished himself as one of the few theologians to address this imbalance by preaching every day of the week on Hebrew scripture, and then reading from the gospels on the Lord's Day when the Lord's Supper was served.[10] This allowed him to include readings from both testaments.

European immigrants to North America enjoyed the freedom to make more changes in the way they worshipped, and, once they arrived on these shores, that sense of freedom only expanded. New England Puritans were the first of many groups to reject the worship format that had become the European norm. Determined to purify the faith even further, the Puritans reconfigured the liturgy and abandoned what remained of the festive parts of the traditional Christian calendar. They were so adamant about this in the sixteenth and seventeenth century that it was not uncommon for Puritans to impose fines on colonists who celebrated Christmas and Easter. The ability to flaunt tradition made the New World a breeding ground for all kinds of religious experimentation. The frontier churches avoided lectionaries because they associated them with "popery." In the seventeenth and eighteenth centuries, many Protestant ministers believed that the Holy Spirit would offer the best influence in choosing preaching texts. To this day, many churches in the Free Church Tradition—African American, non-denominational Christian and Evangelical—eschew the lectionary's format, preferring to encourage preachers to rely on the passages that the Lord lays on their hearts and minds. This habit

10. Interview, Allen.

of pastors praying for a weekly sermon text was the norm in many Protestant churches throughout the nineteenth and early twentieth centuries. The freedom to choose a preaching text was well established and a cherished right that was long associated with freedom of the pulpit.

The nineteenth century witnessed a revival of liturgical rigor in Europe, and, by the twentieth century, many Protestant churches were influenced by an ecumenical spirit, which caused them to reconsider the merits of the lectionary. Vatican II (in 1963) promoted an ecumenical exchange in which Roman Catholics learned more about Protestant worship and *vice versa.* In the twenty-five years after the *Constitution on the Sacred Liturgy* (1963) more changes happened in Roman Catholic liturgy than in the four hundred previous years. The biggest change was the transition from the Latin mass to the vernacular, but other changes included the introduction of congregational singing, and a greater focus on preaching in the mass. The Roman Catholic lectionary began to use scripture translated into contemporary English instead of the King James translation.

The New Revised Common Lectionary

Riding the wave of this ecumenical fervor, the *New Revised Common Lectionary* was developed and came to widespread use in Lutheran, Methodist, Episcopal, Presbyterian, American Baptist, Disciples of Christ, Reformed Church and United Church of Christ congregations. Among the preachers in churches with a more fundamentalist and free-church traditions – including Southern Baptists, Pentecostals, and non-denominational Evangelicals – this trend never gained much traction, because they put such a premium on the process by which the Holy Spirit inspired their pastors' preaching texts. At the other end of the theological spectrum, Unitarian Universalists were increasingly dominated by humanists in the early twentieth century, and so, in time, Bible readings became optional and more often were neglected in favor of secular poems and other literature.

Starting in 1961 there were conversations about merging many Protestants into one mainline denomination; the effort, under the aegis of The Consultation on Church Union, known as COCU, brought together representatives of the Protestant Episcopal Church, the United Methodist Church, The Presbyterian Church USA, and the United Church of Christ. These four major Protestant denominations eventually invited six other denominational representatives to further explore whether there was any potential in this idea. While their 1970 Plan of Union was not ultimately successful, these high-level conversations set the stage for sharing worship resources, particularly for developing a common lectionary. Widespread disappointment around a failed vision for unity may have sparked enthusiasm for a common lectionary.[11]

After the culmination of two decades of ecumenical conversation and debate, the Consultation on Church Texts was constituted in the mid-1960s and chaired by Horace Allen. In 1983 they produced the *New Revised Common Lectionary,* and finalized it in 1992. What distinguished the *New Revised Common Lectionary* from other collections of sacred readings was its adherence to the core belief that it was necessary to organize worship around the theological framework of the incarnation. Readings were chosen to promote the understanding that God was present in human life, in the person and story of Jesus Christ, and that Christ was the incarnate Word sent by God into the world.

Coming as it did on the heels of a small but important ecumenical study by Roman Catholics and Protestants, entitled *Baptism Eucharist and Ministry* (published in 1981 and widely distributed among mainline Protestant clergy), the *New Revised Common Lectionary* began to garner fresh attention and then widespread use in many mainline Protestant churches. While Episcopal, Anglican, and Lutheran Churches had been accustomed to using the lectionary for organizing worship for some time, in the early 1980s this

11. Allen noted that, "At that time the Anglican Church in Great Britain proposed a lectionary based on the Trinity, but it proved to be an artificial construct, because the model obscured the incarnation and so baffled worshippers that it fell into disuse."

habit was beginning to gain ground in congregations aligned with the Presbyterian Church USA, The United Church of Christ, and The United Methodist Church. Swept up in the ecumenical fervor that influenced mainline Protestantism, the early 1980s was a watershed time for the *New Revised Common Lectionary*.

Summary

Though worship traditions appear to be well established, they are by no means static, and never have been. Since the time when the first followers of Jesus began to define their faith as distinct from ancient Judaism, the variety of Christian churches and ways to worship has been staggering. The Church of Jesus Christ has never been monolithic or single-minded when it comes to worship, and the pattern of history shows that part of the success of the church has been its ability to accept change and offer a panorama of expressions of faith. The expressions subscribed to in local congregations were often determined by local customs and the individual experiences of believers around the world. If anything has been constant in the history of worship, it has been the elements of change and adaptation. When times changed, so too did the needs of the people, and there is plenty of evidence that worship evolved to meet these needs.

Throughout church history, worship patterns have adjusted to practical concerns as well as sacred considerations. Although new scholarship points to the lectionary's long-standing tradition—particularly if you subscribe to Spong's theory—this very scholarship also offers insight into how to read the gospels more accurately, rather than to lock the lectionary in place going forward. Spong's and Meyers's theories offer possible insights into the historical use of the gospels, and further evidence that the lectionary has had a significant impact on the church historically, but that history informs us about the past and does not necessarily make definitive claims on the present or the future.

If we look at the history of the church, what we learn is that the church has never existed in a vacuum, but it has always been enmeshed in a creative tension between making an imprint on the culture and reacting to the issues and events of the day. From well before the time of Jesus, the habit of reading scripture and inter-preting it in communities of faith has brought people back every week to hear more. Evolving patterns of Christian worship have included a series of small steps and moderate course corrections, as well as periods of enormous upheaval. Our questions today about how to design and lead meaningful contemporary worship fall squarely into this tradition. While the lectionary readings have a time-honored tradition that spans centuries of worship, and shapes religious time in meaningful ways, it is a system that poses its own set of challenges to contemporary religious leaders who seek to make the messages of faith relevant to today's audiences.

2

New Worship for a New Day

TODAY, THERE IS A widespread concern among clergy and leaders of mainline Protestant churches about the decline in church participation and attendance. Over the last three decades this decline has been dramatic. The statistics demonstrate a drop in church attendance for several decades now, with the accumulated effect of diminished participation in all mainline Protestant denominations. Since the 1960s the declines have been consistent across the board from Episcopalians to Presbyterians, Lutherans to United Methodists. Recent polls also show continued decline even since 1991.[1] *The New York Times* reported in October 2012 that, for the first time since pollsters have been tracking religious affiliation of Americans, a new poll from the Pew Forum on Religion and Public Life showed evidence that fewer than forty percent, well less than half of Americans, attend any church at all or even identify as Protestant, marking a precipitous decline over the last five decades.[2] Pew reported further that one-fifth of the US public, and

1. Barna, "Study of Religious Changes."
2. Pew, "'Nones' on the Rise."

fully one-third of respondents under thirty years of age, have no religious affiliation at all.

It is hard to know exactly how to interpret these trends. Perhaps this change is a correction more than an aberration. It may simply reflect the reestablishment of a balance that was tipped in the middle of the last century when the pendulum tilted toward religious participation in the aftermath of two world wars. This trend of decline may seem more pronounced because it follows on the heels of a surge in church attendance and enthusiasm for religion that accompanied the aftermath of World War II. However, this shift is reconfiguring the ecclesiastical landscape; it has caused churches to close and denominational leaders to rethink how to organize congregational life. The shift has raised many questions about whether it is time to call for major reorganization of church life and worship.

In the first chapter I examined the history of worship and provided an overview of worship patterns within the Judeo-Christian tradition. Throughout the history of worship, we see times when societal upheaval corresponded to liturgical innovation, and other times when worship patterns proved to be remarkably stable. Today, Christian worship is one of the few aspects of modern life that has not changed very much in recent generations; indeed, worship has remained remarkably constant for centuries. Worshippers today who read from the King James Version of the Bible, for example, are reading scripture in an English translation that was developed five hundred years ago, and many of the patterns of speech in that translation reflect the linguistic patterns from a vastly different era in human history. Many modern clergy still wear vestments that have their roots in the Middle Ages. Church music often comes from the work of classical composers from three and four centuries ago. The pipe organ originated in Greece in the third century BCE and has been used in worship since the twelfth century CE. The vast majority of hymns sung in services today include words and music made popular decades, even centuries ago.

It may be that one of the things that attracted people to worship in the last century was the fact that this hour of worship had a timeless quality that was reassuring. Yet times of change, like this one, offer church leaders the opportunity to step back and reconsider the messages we convey consciously, and unconsciously, in worship. Given the plummeting statistics on worship attendance today, there is very little downside to examining all aspects of Christian worship services. In the Middle Ages, when preaching enjoyed new popularity, it was suddenly necessary to put pews in churches for the first time. While it changed the experience of worship quite dramatically, that change was needed to captivate a larger audience. It seems the time has come to question whether worship, as we know it, is still effective at reaching and inspiring our audience today.

Any evaluation of current church decline must examine the sermons. We need to question whether there is something about today's sermons that is either contributing to the steady decline or failing to reverse it. Preaching is one of the oldest styles of communication still in practice today. It is one of the few forms of communication that has not changed very much over the centuries. The Bible describes scenes in synagogues and open air meeting spaces where rabbis, prophets, and apostles talked about faith and interpreted scripture, which shows that the pattern of sharing faith by means of a formal talk has three-thousand years of tradition behind it. But the Bible was written in an age when oratory was highly esteemed. Greco-Roman history is full of examples of political leaders, philosophers, and noted teachers who built their reputation through their oratory. But, communication has changed dramatically, especially in the last century. While oratory still has its place in political conventions, official state gatherings, and religious assemblies, these moments for speeches are fewer and further between. Religious leaders are not immune to the effects of such widespread societal change. Given the pace of modern communication, and the way telecommunications have transformed life as we know it, anyone who preaches regularly needs to be concerned about how to keep their sermons pertinent to contemporary questions of faith, and how to deliver sermons in ways that engage a modern audience. Failure to do so may alienate people further and make our churches even less relevant.

Most modern worshippers have grown accustomed to the new pace of technology. A vast majority of the people who sit in our pews have a cell phone in their pocket, which they will check after the worship service (or during it if they are bored or summoned by an urgent message). These small hand-held informational devices connect worshippers to the worldwide web, to Wikipedia, and to dozens of apps that can amuse or inform. One byproduct of having easy access to so many communication outlets is that most people in churches today have a low tolerance for boredom. That is both a curse and a blessing. It provides strong impetus to make preaching fresh and engaging. No preacher has the luxury of delivering sermons that are stale, rote, or irrelevant. Preaching needs to address the burning questions in a parishioner's mind *and* heart. The hidden blessing is that even with all this technology, many people are left seeking spiritual sustenance and authentic human community in a world where they may feel lonely, or even isolated, as they talk to friends in cyberspace. The pace of modern life leaves many wondering where to find traditions that will offer stability, and whether they articulate this need or not, they do respond to wisdom that has stood the test of time, like that which is found in the Bible or in the Christian tradition. Many people are searching for a depth of experience that internet and television do not offer. My experience is that many modern folks will attend worship and make it a priority in a busy schedule if the worship touches them or answers their questions of faith. Modern audiences will also vote with their feet if they find the messages rote, predictable, or irrelevant.

The other curious part of this picture of mainline Protestant decline is that even in a time of widespread loss of members, some churches are growing and thriving. In fact, not all Protestant churches are losing members. Some have enjoyed enormous growth. In pondering these questions over the last fifteen years, I designed my own informal pilgrimage to churches known for their successful and lively worship centers. In 1998 I started with a trip to Orange County, California to hear Rick Warren preach at Saddleback Church. Saddleback is world-renowned as a mega-church that Warren started from scratch. The story of how Warren conceived of planting the Saddleback church in Orange County is contained in his bestseller, *The Purpose Driven Church*.[3] Though Warren is an Evangelical pastor with a fundamentalist theology, what he describes in his book is an administrative style and approach that are not confined to, or even connected to, any ideological province. His church has thrived by targeting the "unchurched" (those people who are not attending any organized religious institution), and then researching, through surveys and interviews, the reasons that people in this target market have eschewed organized religion. Warren shaped a worship experience that addressed the stated needs of these people. After eighteen months of researching the people in Orange County who had avoided organized religion, Warren created a church experience that was less formal than most church services, because his data told him his audience did not want a church with traditional architecture, or a minister in a long robe, or an organist playing a pipe organ. His light-filled space has a casually dressed choir that sings soft rock Christian music, accompanied by a band. Warren wears his signature Hawaiian shirt, and people sit through a service that is a full hour and a half long each week. In California, Warren discovered that people wanted a less formal style of worship, but had no problem staying longer than an hour. Armed with marketing data, Warren created a worship experience that grew for over twenty years, and now he has a church today where twenty thousand worshippers gather at several different services every weekend. His successful experiment provides some perspective on the current Protestant decline, and has caused me to question whether it would be possible to learn from his experience and utilize those lessons.

One Sunday in May, I travelled to Orange County and attended two worship services to learn more about how Saddleback has made Christian worship user-friendly. The worship center accommodated three thousand people, but the use of screens

3. Warren, *Purpose Driven Church.*

projecting images of the pastor created an intimacy that the space and crowd belied. I found it interesting to note that the sermon topic that day was not particularly theological in any way. Warren used an example from *Newsweek Magazine*, along with some mainstream psychological advice about family life and communicating with your spouse. I was curious and stayed through two services, back to back, to get a feel for how the morning would unfold. The sermon that day, which was repeated at each service, was part of a series on family life. A large crowd attended each service and people were enthusiastic and attentive in both worship sessions. Following worship, people could buy a recorded version of the sermon and the church seemed to be doing a brisk business selling these recordings to those eager to hear the message again.

My experience was so informative that I was eager to investigate other churches known for their growth, their innovative worship, and their ability to buck the trend of Protestant decline. This informal odyssey included trips to Trinity United Church of Christ in Chicago; Mars Hill in Grand Rapids, Michigan; Riverside Church in New York City, and All Souls Unitarian Universalist in Tulsa, Oklahoma (the largest UU congregation in the United States). I enrolled in a workshop on church growth with Mike Piazza, founder of the Cathedral of Hope in Dallas, Texas, and learned about how he started his forty-five hundred member congregation whose target market is gay and lesbian worshippers in Dallas. What I discovered in these thriving churches were worship services that had an energy and an excitement that were palpable. Many of these churches had experimented with worship until they had developed a style and format that were successful for them.

In all these visits and conversations with successful church leaders, I was trying to discover what made some churches able to successfully reach modern people of faith and attract them to worship. What I learned was that churches committed to offering energetic worship, even when that meant changing the way they conduct worship, have not suffered the loss of membership characteristic of our current mainline Protestant decline. In many cases these churches have not only maintained members, but they have expanded, added services, and outgrown their buildings. I also discovered that successful churches, from Evangelical Christians to Unitarian Universalists, were addressing contemporary religious questions in their worship services. More to the point, they might be miles apart ideologically, but they shared a commitment to relevant preaching. In my own informal survey of successful churches, I discovered many preachers using sermon series, and I was hard-pressed to find pastors using the *Revised Common Lectionary,* certainly not exclusively.[4]

From Saddleback to Mars Hill to All Souls, these large churches had attracted people from a variety of faiths and even no faith background at all. People were coming to worship because they found the preaching connected to their lives today. My experience at Mars Hill was particularly telling.

Mars Hill is a church that occupies an abandoned shopping mall. It is not well-marked and it is hard to see any signs that indicate there is a church in this mall, except that, on this particular Sunday, all the cars in the region were headed to the same parking lot, and there were plenty of them. On entering the building, it was obvious to me that the outside signage was the only haphazard quality of the church. Inside of its humble exterior was a highly organized venture, with a genuinely open and friendly atmosphere. Information materials and snacks were all easily available, but people were easygoing, and there was a sense of calm and order everywhere.

The mall space had been retrofitted for Church School, nursery, offices, and a mammoth sanctuary space that accommodated three thousand people who sat in folding chairs on four sides of a raised platform. The lighting made the space almost seem cozy. Large screens above the platform projected images of the preacher, as well as quotes from the sermon and pictures to reinforce his message. The preacher—dressed informally like the crowd, in a shirt and blue jeans—clearly commanded the respect of his

4. The exception to this was The Cathedral of Hope in Dallas, which has a more formal liturgy, but they offer such a rich musical pageantry in the services that it really works for them to use the lectionary.

audience, who appreciated his humor and seemed genuinely engaged in the sermon.

One anecdote from my experience was particularly telling. When I found my seat I introduced myself to the family beside me, a couple with two teenagers. I asked them how long they had been attending this church and they told me they had been coming weekly for seven years. When I inquired about why they liked it, the father replied that he liked the preaching. "In the beginning we came for our children, and we were pleasantly surprised to see how much they liked it, but now I come for myself too. I never felt like I understood the Bible at other churches. Rob Bell brings the Bible down to our level, and we can understand what he is saying. The Bible finally makes sense to me; the Bible never made sense to me before I came here."

As worship began, I realized that the service had fewer elements than many I had attended. With one song by a rock singer, no unison prayers, and no hymns or offertory, the sermon was the centerfold of this service and I listened intently, given the testimonial offered with frank ease by the people to my left. To my surprise, Bell preached a sermon on forgiveness very similar to one I had delivered in my church a few months before. He even used some of the same illustrations, same points, and similar ideas.

Now, I have discovered that sermons on forgiveness elicit one of the biggest responses of sermons on any topic all year long. Sermons on this topic touch a real place of spiritual need, and it has become my practice to be sure to preach about forgiveness at least once a year. But forgiveness is a complex topic, and when you preach one sermon a year you can only go so deep. At Mars Hill, I discovered that Bell had been preaching on this topic all month, for four weeks in a row. Listening to him preach the fourth sermon in his series on forgiveness, it became clear how much more effective it was to introduce the topic, develop the topic, and allow for the congregation to take time to really absorb the lessons, especially when a topic is multi-layered and carries such deep personal implications. Preaching a series, instead of a single sermon, on a serious subject is more effective, because it allows the audience the opportunity to reflect on the lessons and process their own experiences over time, as the series progresses. Bell's approach allowed the congregation to ruminate on the topic over several weeks. His final illustration emphasized this point. He told the story of the Amish community where the people forgave a gunman after the school house massacre at Nickel Mines Elementary School in 2006. It was the same illustration I had used in my annual sermon on forgiveness. What I realized, as Bell spoke, was that his congregation was better prepared to hear such a dramatic example of forgiveness after four weeks of thinking about the topic, and it was clear how much more effective it was at the end of a series than at the end of a single sermon. Reading through copies of Bell's other sermons in his series on forgiveness, I saw how he was able to lay the groundwork throughout the series, and reinforce the points of his messages week after week.

What I discovered in my journey to various churches around the country was that so many of these thriving churches were attracting audiences that were enthusiastic about worship, and about the sermons they listened to each week. The preachers in these places were devoting a larger percentage of the worship service to the sermon, and people responded positively. At Mars Hill, the sermon was the main event, and at Saddleback, Warren preached for a full fifty minutes while people in his audience took notes. Oratory in these places had not diminished in stature at all, but the congregations in these churches were enthusiastic about worship, even about longer sermons (by today's standards), because their preachers were connecting the Bible messages to the current questions of faith that people are asking today. In almost every case, these churches were preaching from themes that they identified in the Bible, but they were not taking their texts from the lectionary. The practice of using sermon series that addressed a single topic was standard.

When it comes to preaching style or content, most mainline Protestants cannot copy either the Evangelical mega-church model or the Unitarian Universalists' format. Fundamentalists are too theologically conservative, and Unitarian Universalists do not use

Bible lessons or scripture enough for most Protestant churches. But the creativity that these churches have demonstrated in shaping worship is not tied to any theological outlook. This simple fact made me think that any of us might borrow part of the spirit of ingenuity evident in these growing churches today, on the conservative and progressive ends of the theological spectrum, and apply it to our own worship services.

These trips were eye opening; they made me question my own preaching style and wonder whether the lectionary was a help or a hindrance. For two decades I had used the *New Revised Common Lectionary*. At the start of my ministry, using the lectionary was a good discipline, and it increased my Biblical bandwidth. However, after eighteen years and six preaching cycles of using the lectionary exclusively, I realized it had some real limitations, and it had become increasingly restrictive, even cumbersome at times. Central to the problems with using the lectionary are the assumptions inherent in that model. The lectionary preaching model makes several assumptions about the worshipping audience. For example, all lectionaries are based on the assumption that weekly worship attendance is the norm. Also, churches that use the *New Revised Common Lectionary* exclusively assume that their audience has a basic understanding of the rationale for the lectionary and its theological approach.

In my experience, none of these assumptions are reliably true today. In the first place, there are many church members who consider themselves active and may not attend worship weekly. New polls and research shows that the norms for church attendance have been shifting over the last two decades. For several decades following World War II, standards for regular worship attendance were weekly worship on Sundays, but the definition of church attendance has changed. Currently, the broad definition of a regular church attendee is someone who attends a worship service three out of eight weekends. "Maybe a pastor used to be able to count on seeing someone every week, but what's now happening is that people's lives are busier and they're attending more infrequently."[5]

5. Barnes and Lowry, "7 Startling Facts."

The research on church attendance is somewhat contradictory on this point. For seventy years, Gallup has reported that 40 percent of the population has claimed that they attend worship weekly, but researchers attribute this to the "halo effect", the perception that church attendance is desirable and impressive, so it is more widely reported than is accurate. Even the gradual secularization of the nation, which church leaders have noticed for years, has not "eliminated the perceived social desirability of going to church."[6] However, my own perceptions of shifting church attendance, while admittedly anecdotal, point to trends that undermine even the best intentions to attend weekly worship. More Middle Class Americans have Sunday morning conflicts and choices that compete with worship—work obligations, children's sports events, family events, personal travel, retreats, and charity runs all compete with worship and prove too irresistible to pass up. This means that when the sermon is based on scripture readings that follow a weekly progression, modern worshipers who come as often as they can, but perhaps only once or twice a month, lose the context of the sermon and miss the weekly connections. If the sermon message is not easily understood, and worshipers don't follow its logic, then they may not return, because today's worshippers have many choices on Sunday morning.

In the computer industry, people have come to put a premium on messages that are "intuitive." As a result, modern audiences expect that, as they navigate the culture, they will find messages everywhere that are easy to understand; many people have no patience with anything that is too confusing or time-consuming. To attract a modern audience, churches must have messages that are easily understandable to the novice churchgoer as well as the veteran.

The lectionary presents the Christian message in a fairly complex way, which is not intuitive to newcomers. The organization of

6. Paulson "Americans Claim." In 2012 Pew Researchers discovered that among "religiously affiliated Americans who say that religion is at least somewhat important in their lives," but attend worship services infrequently, 24% cite personal priorities including 16% who say they are too busy. Lipka, "What Surveys Say about Worship Attendance."

readings offers a calendar approach to the story of Jesus. This story begins in Advent and goes on through Pentecost, and it assumes that today's congregations comprehend that they are accompanying Jesus through his birth, life, death, resurrection, and ascension as they celebrate Advent, Christmas, Epiphany, Lent, Easter and Pentecost. Many of these theological assumptions, while they may make sense to clergy, befuddle the ordinary listener. And so the lectionary, which was intended to offer a window into the Christian story, has become a wall for many people.

Another piece of the puzzle is the changing audience in many mainline Protestant churches. Current trends indicate that there is very little denominational brand loyalty among worshippers today.[7] So, in many churches, the membership includes people from every religious background as well as those who have had no experience in a church or spiritual community. Even if one were determined to give all church participants a crash course in the theological underpinnings of the lectionary, it would be a daunting task, given the scope of religious experiences represented in most congregations every week.

In his book *The Purpose Driven Church*, Rick Warren offers advice for ministers about how to survey your target market when planting a church, and how to listen to the audience that they hope to reach. His data was pioneering work in 1996, and it helped him identify a target audience for his church. While it sounds to some church people that this was more like a business plan than church evangelism, this target market helped Warren's Saddleback Church be clear about its goals and objectives. In the first chapter of his book, Warren describes the results of his survey information in Orange County, and creates a composite caricature of the people he hopes to attract—someone he named "Saddleback Sam." The survey information Warren gleaned told him that Saddleback Sam avoided religion because he did not like organ music, clergy vestments, or stained glass windows. What Warren's experience

---

7. A study in 2009 by *Gray Matter Research and Consulting* found that Protestants are no more loyal to their denominations than they are to their brand of toothpaste.

suggests is that there is evidence that churches increase their chances of success when they really pay attention to the preferences of the people they seek to attract. The price we pay for clinging to the relatively unimportant vestiges of the past, like where we find our scripture readings, is that it may be causing us to lose the opportunity to share the faith at all.

On February 7, 2012, National Public Radio's "All Things Considered" featured a story on Jefferson Bethke, whose video on YouTube, entitled "Why I Hate Religion, but Love Jesus," had attracted well over eighteen million hits. The reporter highlighted the ease with which anyone can get attention on YouTube. In an Op-ed piece for the *New York Times,* David Brooks dismissed Bethke as another immature rebel.[8] What the media analysis missed here is that Bethke hit a nerve, especially among younger adults and youth. In Bethke's rap on Jesus he criticized the hypocrisy of the church, which may make it very easy for those of us who work in this institution to feel defensive. But Bethke's viral video may also hold a message for church leaders. He may be telling us that it is time to reevaluate the way we present and package our stories of faith. Bethke seems to say that he is interested in getting to know Jesus Christ, but not in the ways in which most churches package the man from Galilee.

Reporting in the *Christian Century,* Adam Copeland describes a Christian mission outreach to young adults in Fargo, North Dakota, that has enjoyed surprising success. Copeland is a director and developer of Project F-M, a program based in Fargo and in Moorhead, Minnesota. Within the metro area of Fargo and Moorhead, Copeland reported that, although there were scores of vital mainline Protestant churches, none of the 45,000 young adults, who comprised one-quarter of the population, were connected to any of them. While there were plenty of choices for someone seeking a house of worship, Copeland discovered a complete mismatch between what these churches offered, and what young adults were seeking.[9] So Adam Copeland started Theology

8. Brooks, "How to Fight."

9. Copeland, "No Need," 12–13.

Pub, a very different ministry from even those "aimed" at young or emerging adults in established churches. He saw his role not as the shepherd of his flock, but more as one of the sheep. A fellow seeker himself, he "listens a lot and talk[s] very little" to emerging adults who would never go into an organized church, but who want to talk about faith in a pub. Eschewing the role of "expert," Copeland warns that anyone designing a program with young adults must "allow participants to listen to one another, to form friendships, and to relax in the beauty of holy conversation."[10]

Ideas about changing the worship space in such a dramatic fashion are way beyond the scope of this book, and for many churches they represent a shift that would be seen as "pushing the envelope" too far. But the common thread that connects all of these examples is that creative change most appropriately commences with a decided commitment to listen to the people who are disappointed in organized religion, in order to hear what the concerns or criticisms really are.

One exercise in listening that made a lasting impression on me took place on a very cold Tuesday in January 2012. As part of a seminary class about the ministry needs of young adults (those between the ages of eighteen and thirty), we were assigned to take a survey to a place where we could find a large group of young adults who might provide information about how they feel about religion, spirituality, and faith participation. Several of my classmates decided to go to college campuses, but I took my surveys to JP Licks, a popular ice cream shop in a Boston neighborhood known for its young adult clientele. This ice cream shop has earned the status of community center; even in the dead of winter it was crowded. The process of taking this survey about religion to strangers between the ages of eighteen and thirty years old was not one I relished, as I had assumed it would be met with disinterest, or possibly hostility. To my surprise, I found so many people willing to participate in my project that some of *them* started recruiting their friends to fill out my form. In less than an hour I had exhausted my supply of surveys and found it necessary to get additional copies. After two

10. Ibid.

hours, I had spoken to over thirty young adults—none of them attended church services, but all of them had information to share about faith and their opinions about God.

Many of the surveys confirmed that young adults do not distinguish among religious traditions. People who identify as former Roman Catholics enjoy the spiritual effects of Thai Chi, yoga, and meditation. Across many faiths or none, young adults told me that music offered a reliable spiritual connection. Art was often cited as an avenue for religious expression. In his book *Emerging Adulthood,* Peter Arnett identifies this trend in his chapter on "Sources of Meaning: Make-Your-Own Religions." Arnett cites a man named Carl who identifies as a Christian, but seamlessly incorporates the *Star Wars* notion of "The Force" into his theology. This example illustrates the fluid way that young and emerging adults pick their beliefs from a smorgasbord of religious notions in a variety of faiths and popular culture. While it might seem unsettling to some theological sticklers, it points to a very creative energy in the search for faith among young adults.[11] What surprised me most were the responses I saw to one question on the survey, "When was the last time you talked to anyone about God?" I learned that most respondents to my survey had talked about God within the week. Over and over again, I recognized that the topic of faith was a live one for respondents. In many ways, I suppose I should not have been surprised. Certainly, Arnett demonstrates that young adults are serious about their life goals and are no strangers to self-reflection. While they may be abandoning the institutional church in droves, clearly this survey tapped a wellspring of interest in faith.

When returning her survey to me, one woman made a point of introducing herself, shaking my hand, and offering her blessing on my work. She had been all alone at her table, working with a coffee cup and laptop—something in her body language and demeanor made me cautious about even approaching her. So her desire to shake hands, and her gratitude for being asked to take the survey, took me completely by surprise. Another young man stayed for an extra half hour after his shift behind the counter to

11. Arnett, *Emerging Adulthood*, 171.

fill out the survey, and write at length about his spiritual journey. When he was done, I thanked him and he left quickly, explaining that he was running late for his second job. It was a cold night, and so when I offered him a ride he took it. All the way to the subway station he talked enthusiastically about his artwork and how his paintings were full of material drawn from the lives of the saints, which he learned about as a child in the Roman Catholic Church.

The vast majority of the respondents had grown up under the influence of some church, but, without exception, now found religious institutions utterly irrelevant. While not officially religious in any organized or institutional way, many of the respondents were engaged in vital spiritual journeys, and committed to putting their faith into action. They sought moral and spiritual mentors, and they asked questions about life's meaning and purpose that were fundamentally religious in nature. Reading the surveys convinced me that the church would be much richer if we could find a way to connect to their causes, and allow their energy to influence us. However, the growing gap between the way most churches express faith and the spiritual questions that interest young adults is a problem for the church, and probably also a loss for young adults, who seek communities in which to explore their faith and spirituality. The danger is that, within one generation, churches may become irrelevant.

Times of change present the Church with opportunities to reinvent itself. From my perspective, any real change in the Protestant church must involve a thorough review of the content and form of worship. In December 2011, Eric Weiner wrote an Op-ed piece in the *New York Times*, where he said, "We need a Steve Jobs of religion, someone who can invent not a new religion but a new way of being religious. This new way would be straightforward and unencumbered and absolutely intuitive. It would celebrate doubt, encourage experimentation, and allow you to talk about God without embarrassment."[12]

Several years ago, four families were joining my church. They had been searching for a church for their children, and then had

12. Weiner, "Undecided."

been surprised to discover that they were also engaged in an adult quest to know more about God. Two of the adults had never been baptized. Since baptism is a requirement for membership in our church, they came to talk to me about what this sacrament meant before consenting to it. They seemed to seek my re-assurance that we did not subscribe to some of the more traditional views of baptism. I suggested that their baptisms were more like Jesus' had been than they might have realized. For him, this moment marked the start of a new and deeper chapter in the life of faith, and so did theirs. Baptism was less about being cleansed from sin and more about their new faith commitment. This kind of interpretation resonated with them in ways that substitutionary atonement never had, and probably never would. I see these two individuals as part of a new trend that may be emerging in our churches.

Eric Weiner made a wise observation when he suggested that our churches need to be more intuitive; at the very least, they need to be user-friendly. We need to find ways to package the faith material so that it makes sense to the people who are seeking spiritual nurture today. The Apple Company that Jobs created has thrived in a spirit of experimentation, collaboration, and user-friendliness. Any church that figures out how to incorporate even a fraction of that spirit of adventure into the theological discussion will bring a new energy to the congregation. Any church that begins to focus on listening to the people who are not in the pews, along with those who are, will learn a lot about what modern people of faith are seeking, and why droves of people who grew up in a church are staying away from religious institutions today.

Summary

I began my work as a minister when I completed seminary in 1981, and so my entire ministry and time in the pulpit have been lived under the influence of the *New Revised Common Lectionary.* I entered the profession when mainline Protestants were discovering the lectionary and adhering to it with the fervor of new converts. I was no exception, and my preaching was steeped in it, exclusively, for eighteen years. Ironically, it was this discipline that introduced me to some of the richer portions of scripture, and expanded my biblical horizons, but it also has made me aware of the weaknesses in the *New Revised Common Lectionary*.

Leading worship today has taught me that there is a new criterion for sermons and for choosing scripture readings. In a time when worship patterns are shifting, and many Protestant churches are declining, one important criterion for worship is that the sermons and the liturgy need to be so easily understood that people can comprehend the message immediately, and will want to return again. For example, when I created the worship bulletins for many decades, the date appeared on the cover along with a lectionary designation about where the calendar date fell within the liturgical year. It might say, "June 4, Third Sunday After Pentecost," or "January 11, Second Sunday of Epiphany." We might as well have put a secret code on the worship bulletin, which communicated that newcomers had entered a building with its own language, and that they were outsiders who would have to learn a lot before they felt comfortably included in the circle of those who knew what was going on.

As we have done for centuries now, I believe churches are being called on to rethink the way we organize worship in order to meet the requirements of a new set of challenges, including a new need for communicating the messages of faith.

3

The Elephant in the Room
Looking at the Assumptions in the Lectionary

MY PILGRIMAGE TO GROWING churches made a lasting impression on me, and challenged me to reevaluate my preaching style and content. These trips drew my attention to an unlikely convergence. Both Evangelical Christians and Unitarian Universalists were using thematic sermon series effectively. Though the messages from these two kinds of pulpits could not be more different, the way that they delivered their message was strikingly similar. This strange realization made me wonder what was going on. Evangelicals and Unitarians had little in common, theologically, and were at opposite poles in terms of their regard for the Bible but these churches were preaching with themes in similar ways. I realized that both churches were targeting new members, and seeking to attract people who came from other faiths, or none at all. Both Evangelical Christians and UU's had revised their services, attempting to make them more intuitive for an audience that had no experience in their churches. These congregations on the far right and the far left both discovered that preaching styles needed to be reexamined and revised. Though they had been led down very different theological paths, they had adopted similar worship goals and arrived at common conclusions about the efficacy and importance of preaching with themes.

This realization makes me wonder how effective lectionary preaching is, even in mainline Protestant churches. It raises the question of whether worshippers in any of the churches really understand why the lectionary readings have been chosen and where they come from. Are these readings doing a good job of teaching the tenets of the Christian faith? Does the lectionary help or hinder preachers' attempts to attract new members and reach their audience with a relevant message? The answers to these questions may vary from church to church. But, in my experience, even bright and attentive parishioners often had almost no clue about why we were reading a particular scripture lesson from one week to the next. They could not see a connection between the passages assigned from the Old and New Testaments. They regarded the choice of readings as somewhat random most weeks, with the exception of Christmas and Easter. One man said, "We had no idea what the readings were or where they came from. They seemed to be dropped out of the blue and took us by surprise each week." No amount of explanation seemed to bridge the gaps, and sadly the lectionary became a form of obfuscation for many worshipers, rather than a window to the stories in the Bible.

In this chapter, I will be discussing the *New Revised Common Lectionary.* While this is one of the most recent versions, and the one with which I am most familiar, this chapter also evaluates the lectionary tradition, and critiques some of the assumptions in the lectionaries that have been used for centuries, in an effort to step away from this tradition and see it in a different light.

It takes time to learn to work with the *New Revised Common Lectionary.* Preachers who use the lectionary acclimate themselves to the set of assumptions that the lectionary makes about the Bible and theology. Many of these assumptions have been learned in seminary and are re-enforced as a pastor builds his or her craft as a preacher. Thus, it is hard to recognize those assumptions because they have become engrained in a preacher's mindset as the cycles of scripture unfold each year. It takes a certain distance to see that the lectionary is not value neutral, and never has been.

I believe it is important to re-examine the theological assumptions of the lectionary in order to really evaluate it as a worship tool. At first glance, it may seem that the scripture lessons included in the *New Revised Common Lectionary* represent a sampling of all the important texts culled from various books of the Bible. But, upon closer examination, one discovers that the authors made value judgments about which scripture passages to include, and how to arrange them. Neither the selection of passages, nor their organization within the lectionary framework, is value neutral. It is important to see and understand the bias of the editors of the lectionary.

The *New Revised Common* Lectionary is a statement of faith. As I stated in chapter 1, it organizes worship around the theological framework of the incarnation, and proposes that the way worshippers grasp this truth is by taking a journey of faith through the life of Jesus, from Advent to Pentecost. The choice of scripture—the way the passages are organized and the sequence of them—all support this statement of faith and the worship drama that expresses it. The authors of the lectionary promote the notion that the Hebrew Bible is best seen as a foreshadow of the New Testament. All of the stories about the covenant between God and Israel contained in the Old Testament are a prelude to the new covenant that Jesus embodies and fulfills in the New Testament. The *New Revised Common Lectionary* makes this statement of faith in the readings it chooses, and in the way that it organizes those readings.

The first assumption I will address is the way that the *New Revised Common Lectionary* casts Advent as a time when Christians await the Second Coming of the Lord. This strong theme in the Advent readings is hard for many modern worshippers to understand, because it runs against peoples' expectations for the services leading up to Christmas. After years of preaching Advent sermons, it has been my experience that when I try to use the lectionary during this four-week period, this assumption in the lectionary makes it very difficult to offer an uplifting message.

The lectionary readings place Advent within the theological framework of the coming of a new age, as heralded by the life and prophesy of John the Baptist. Two out of four gospel readings during Advent tell the story of this Baptizer—a gruesome tale of an odd prophet who lived an ascetic life in the wilderness, subsisting on wild honey and locusts. His fanatic preaching earned him a reputation among the faithful, as well as a grisly beheading. While there may be some significant theological reasons to make the John's story prominent during Advent, most people in the pews cannot take this theological leap, and there is little incentive for them to try. They come to church expecting to hear about a sweet little baby born to a world that had lost hope. Instead, through much of Advent, the lectionary offers them a wild-eyed fanatic who dwells at the edge of society. Even the most diligent of clergy is hard-pressed to feed the flock this castor oil when they come expecting Figgie pudding. It might be good for them, but most worshippers refuse to take much of it. Advent proves to be the opposite of a teachable moment when it comes to this particular theological connection.

Another problem with the lectionary during Advent is the way the texts are organized in an effort to create anticipation. All of the readings during the season lead up to the birth of Jesus, but do not tell the story directly. The birth narrative itself unfolds for the first time on Christmas Eve. To strictly preach the lectionary during Advent, a preacher has to avoid mentioning the birth of Jesus until the very last minute. Not only is this a difficult discipline, but it makes no sense to the congregation to avoid what seems to be an open secret, and one that has brought most of them to the service in the first place. But the lectionary makes no reference to the birth until the Fourth Sunday in Advent, as the Gospel reading tells of the Annunciation when the Angel Gabriel visits Mary with news of her impending pregnancy (Matt 1:18–25 or Luke 1:25–38). Though churchgoers in December all know how the story will end on Christmas Eve, the lectionary takes us on a journey of collective amnesia as it outlines the background leading up to Christ's birth, without spoiling the ending until Christmas Eve. This approach might work well in a monastery or convent where people are not exposed to the Christmas story in any other part of their lives. But, in modern society today, people begin to hear Christmas carols like "Silent Night" sung in the malls and supermarkets in October, so the church is left behind when we fail to address the story that is on everybody's mind throughout Advent. Sadly, the subtleties of the lectionary's sense of liturgical order are lost on most worshippers, and they fail to understand why any church would not mention Christmas's culmination until after Advent. Ministers who adhere to the lectionary's assumptions that the season of Christmas begins on Christmas Eve may be missing a real opportunity to talk about the meaning of the birth of Jesus when the crowd is robust and eager for the church's interpretation. Any attempt to maintain suspense throughout this high liturgical season renders preachers out of touch with the people they strive to reach.

There is another, more serious problem with the lectionary and the way it organizes the scripture readings. The editors of the *New Revised Common Lectionary* offered a three-year list of scripture readings.[1] Each week's lections include one psalm, one reading from any of the other books in the Old Testament, one gospel reading, and one reading from Acts or Paul's letters. Simply by the way that it is organized, this framework gives prominence to the New Testament. There are thirty-nine books in the Old Testament and twenty-seven in the New Testament. If you look only at the content of these books, the Old Testament is approximately three times larger than the New Testament. Time spent reading the New Testament is taken at the expense of the Old Testament. In addition, the use of the four gospels and the psalms on a weekly basis gives special prominence to those five books. Old Testament stories are not eliminated entirely during the six months between Advent and Pentecost, but they often take a backseat to the drama of the life of Jesus. While the lectionary does offer an opportunity

1. They offer readings for every day of the year, but for the purposes of my argument here I will just deal with Sunday's selections.

in the three-year cycle to explore many Old Testament passages, the way that they are included in the lectionary sets them up to serve the trajectory and message at the heart of this Christocentric calendar.

Let me illustrate this phenomenon with a closer examination of the lectionary passages listed for the Sundays spanning the time from Advent through Easter. All of the Old Testament stories suggested for Advent in Cycle B, for example, come from the prophet Isaiah, whose writings are used to demonstrate that, whether he realized it or not, the prophet and one of his disciples were predicting the birth of Jesus when they wrote words of comfort to the Israelites exiled in Babylon, and to the recent returnees seeking to rebuild the temple more than five hundred years before Jesus' birth. There is only one Old Testament passage that is not from Isaiah during the four weeks of Advent. That comes on the Fourth Sunday of Advent, and it is Nathan's vision in II Sam 7:1–11. Here, it talks about how God wants King David to build a temple for the Ark of the Covenant so that God can dwell with the people. It would be a very random reference were it not paired that day with the Annunciation in Luke 1:26–34, where Gabriel announces to Mary that she will bear a child, and the implication is that God will once again come to live among the people in a concrete way. Whatever original meaning Nathan's vision might have had ten centuries before Christ's birth, here it is used to serve the purposes of the Christian calendar.

During Epiphany, the Old Testament selections all serve to support the message in the New Testament, too. On the Sunday that recognizes the Baptism of Jesus (Mark 1:4–11) the Old Testament verses come from the story of creation (Gen 1:1–5), which supports the premise that, as Jesus comes into his own and begins his ministry, God is creating the world anew. On the second and third Sundays in the Season of Epiphany, the Old Testament passages tell of the call of Samuel (I Sam 3:1–10), and then the call of Jonah (Jonah 3:1–5,10). It might offer the opportunity to do a short series on vocation, but the reason that these ancient calls are used during these weeks is because they coincide with the arc of the Christian story in the life of Jesus, and this is when the New Testament recounts the calling of the first disciples (Mark 1:14–20). Then, on the fourth Sunday of Epiphany, when Jesus begins his ministry in Capernaum (Mark 1:21–28), the Old Testament reading comes from Deuteronomy, a somewhat random choice taken from a section of the Bible about the Levitical priesthood and the prophets of Israel, except that Moses' words here are: "The Lord your God will raise up for you a prophet from among your own people; you shall heed such a prophet"(Deut 18:15). Presumably, this text has been chosen to demonstrate that Jesus is the new Moses. On the next Sunday, when the lectionary looks at the Transfiguration of Jesus, we hear about an episode when his closest disciples have a mystical experience and envision Jesus transformed into an other-worldly figure, whose garments and body are infused with a heavenly light. The Old Testament reading that day recounts the prophet Elijah's ascension to heaven, riding on an extra-terrestrial chariot.

Then, after the Season of Epiphany, we come to Lent. During Lent, in Cycle B again, the Old Testament passages focus on the theme of covenant: the first Sunday describes God's covenant with Noah after the flood (Gen 9:18–17); the second Sunday in Lent describes God's covenant with Abraham (Gen 17:1–7, 15–16); the third Sunday recounts the Ten Commandments in Exod 20:1–17; and on the fifth Sunday of Lent the passage recalls Jeremiah's words about God making a new covenant with the people (Jer 31:31–34). At this point, it becomes clear that the various covenant stories serve to illustrate that Jesus is the embodiment of the new covenant. This theory is clinched on the fourth Sunday in Lent when the Old and New Testament passages play off of one another. The first comes from the story of Moses holding up a serpent in the wilderness, which God turns to bronze (Num 21:4–9). The New Testament reading for that same day comes from the fourth gospel, where John says that Jesus must be lifted up just as the serpent was lifted up by Moses (John 3:4–21).

From Advent to the Fifth Sunday of Lent, all the Old Testament passages promote and support the theological arc of the Christian story as depicted in the New Testament selections.

Then, from Palm Sunday through Trinity Sunday (a span of nine weeks), no Old Testament passages are listed for readings in worship. During this time, readings from the Book of Acts, with its tales of the early Christian church, supplant all readings from the Old Testament. I have used readings from Cycle B to illustrate this imbalance, but the pattern persists in all three cycles (A, B, and C). That said, one might easily argue that, in Christian churches, it is appropriate to emphasize the New Testament and downplay the Old Testament; however, I believe this systemic imbalance in the lectionary hinders our exposure to the broader range of scriptural resources available in the Old Testament.

A bigger problem with the lectionary is the way that it renders the Old Testament subordinate to the New. The choice of texts in the Hebrew Bible implicitly supports the theological assumption that the Old Testament, the Jews, and Judaism, draw their sole significance from the way that they prepare for Christianity. This is not done in the way it organizes the schedule for readings, but more in the theological decisions that are made by the choice of Old Testament scripture passages to support the message of the gospel reading. Passages from the Prophets are selected in Advent to promote the notion that the birth of Jesus is the fulfillment of the Messianic hope foretold in Jewish prophetic literature. Readings from Isaiah during Advent, for example, assume that the original intention of the prophet was to predict the birth of Jesus of Nazareth. During Lent, when portions from the prophet Zechariah promote the understanding that Zechariah predicted Jesus' entry into Jerusalem, it leads you to assume that Jesus' death was part of the Jewish prophetic legacy. The editors' decision to use Hebrew scripture to illustrate the themes in the New Testament lessons is a loss for Christians, because those who follow the lectionary miss some of the messages in the Old Testament, which stand independently of the issues and ideas in the New Testament. Many of the Old Testament passages have little to do with Jesus, and need no embellishment, but their significance is overlooked, or vastly underrated, because they do not promote the theory at the heart of the lectionary: that the Old Testament story of faith culminates in the life of Jesus.

The choice of Hebrew scripture lessons, the context of these passages in the Christian calendar, and the way that they are paired with gospel or epistle readings, all promote the theory that Hebrew scripture lays the groundwork for the life, death, and resurrection of Jesus Christ. The organization of the readings implies that Jesus is the Messiah for whom the Jews waited for centuries, and that he completes the covenants established originally by Abraham, Moses, and the other patriarchs and prophets. Granted, this is one of the basic tenets of Christian faith; however, this assumption ignores the integrity and original intent of Hebrew scripture.

Let me explain why this is problematic for modern Christian audiences. In the first place, this approach to Hebrew scripture is disrespectful of Jewish thought and theology. It discounts the Hebrew stories of faith and the spiritual resources they offer to Christians, as well as to Jews. Reading the Old Testament as a prelude to the New Testament shortchanges the Judeo-Christian tradition so that Christians forfeit many of the lessons that Jewish writing has for us too. Instead, if Christians strive to read the Old Testament with an eye for the original meaning and intent of the Hebrew authors, we find that the Old Testament offers a treasure trove of insights and instruction about how to live in a faith community, how to confront injustice, and how to journey in faith one's entire life. To read the Old Testament as nothing more than a set-up for the arrival of Jesus Christ is to ignore centuries of wisdom relevant to Christians today.

The second reason why it may be a mistake to view the Old Testament as primarily a background story for the life of Jesus is that Hebrew scripture formed the foundation of Jesus' own faith. As Christians who aspire to follow in Jesus' footsteps, we need to consider his world, and what informed his faith. This is a particularly compelling topic for modern Christians. In his groundbreaking book, *The Search for the Historical Jesus* (1910), Albert Schweitzer brought worldwide attention to a new approach to Christian scholarship. In the late twentieth and early twenty-first centuries, many modern scholars have reexamined Jesus' life by studying Hebrew scripture on its own terms, seeking to discover more about the historical setting of Jesus' life as a Galilean Jew.[2] Any inquiry into Jesus' life and times must include a study of Hebrew scripture on its own terms.

When we strive to follow Jesus it is hard to underestimate the importance of recognizing his Jewishness, and what it meant to him to live in a Jewish community, read the Torah, study scriptures with other Jewish men, and to view the world through a thoroughly Jewish perspective. For too long, Christians have ignored the fact that Jesus was born, lived, and died a Jew. Biblical scholar Amy-Jill Levine makes this point persuasively in her book *The Misunderstood Jew: The Church and the Scandal of The Jewish Jesus*. Writing in *Christian Century*, John Vest summarizes the experience of many Protestants:

> I realized that references to the Old Testament had been largely absent from the evangelicalism of my youth. Yes, I learned the standard Old Testament Sunday school stories- Noah's flood, Moses and the Exodus, Jonah and the big fish, Elijah's prophetic adventures, and David and Goliath. Otherwise, however, I had read only selected quotations used in the New Testament or Christological readings of portions of the prophetic literature. Everything that I had been told was important came from a rather narrow reading of the New Testament. I realized my understanding of salvation had nothing to do with the Old Testament . . . for the most part Jesus had no connection to Judaism and appeared out of nowhere to save us from God's unflinching wrath. . . . Just as the Jesus of evangelicalism often exists in the vacuum of a salvation narrative, the Jesus of my mainline Protestantism often exists in a vacuum of social justice and peacemaking.[3]

2. Albert Schweitzer's book reviews work on the historical Jesus, pointing out that Jesus' image changed with the times, from the seventeenth century on. Schweitzer examined Jesus in light of Jesus' own faith, as part of a late Jewish eschatological movement.

3. Vest, "Reflections," 21.

Vest points out that Christians on the right and the left sides of the theological spectrum have too often ignored Jesus' Jewishness when they overlook the Hebrew Bible, which is the scripture that Jesus memorized and lived by. If we are to truly come to terms with the fullness of who Jesus was and how he saw the world, we will need to study and worship with the scripture that had such a formative effect on his life and ministry.

As I began to move away from the *New Revised Common Lectionary* and started to preach with themes, I made a concerted effort to study the Hebrew Bible so as to honor the integrity of its original message, and looked for themes that spanned both testaments. In lifting the Hebrew Bible to a level of respect often missing in Christian worship, I believe it was possible to reduce the subtle anti-Semitism inherent in the way Christians have been reading and hearing the Hebrew Bible for centuries. What I discovered was that preaching the stories from the Old Testament on their own terms did not diminish the Christian message; if anything, it added a new dimension to the faith in which Jesus himself was nurtured, and fostered a new respect for his people.

I think it is worth noting that the term "Old" Testament itself makes a value judgment about the way scripture fits together. Modern Biblical scholars who are concerned about the long-standing prejudice about Jewish texts inherent in Christianity have tried to address this prejudice by calling the works of scripture that precede the birth of Jesus the "Hebrew Bible." While it may help Christians to respect the primary portion of the Bible on its own terms, I have decided to use traditional language in this book because it reflects common usage.

The third reason why the lectionary treatment of the Old Testament poses a problem for Protestants has to do with the theme of liberation that might arguably be seen as the strongest theme running through both testaments. The story of the Exodus is indeed the formative story at the start of the Biblical narrative, describing the liberation of Hebrew slaves from Egypt, the most powerful empire of the day. The story at the heart of this narrative reveals God's desire to be involved in freeing Hebrew slaves, and aligning

God's self on the side of the least powerful in order to confront the world's powerbrokers. This notion that God can be relied upon to advocate for those seeking liberation becomes the message of hope that drives Jewish faith. Notable scholars like Walter Brueggemann and John Dominic Crossan make the point that the central message of the Bible is to call for people of faith to stand up to powerful empires. From the stories of Genesis through to the ministry of Paul, there is a consistent message about the way that God works in the world, which is on the side of the underdog. The Bible offers ordinary people the hope that the hegemonic power of political and economic empires can always be challenged by people of faith, and that God joins humans in such struggles.

Unfortunately, this theme is too often downplayed, if not systematically overlooked, in the way that the lectionary emphasizes the prophet's prediction of the Messiah. Often taking these prophetic pronouncements out of context, in order to serve the purposes of foreshadowing the ministry of Jesus, the lectionary tradition overlooks those prophet's pronouncements about God's call for justice that confronts the concentrated power in the world's various empires. Ironically, when we respect the Old Testament readings in their original context and see the messages of faith within them, both testaments unfold more organically, and Jesus' resistance against Rome bares remarkable similarities to the way that former prophets railed against Babylon. Oddly enough, if the progression of scripture could be honored and respected for its own integrity within its time and place, it reveals a deeply consistent message. While Jesus may or may not have been the messiah who was predicted by Old Testament visionaries, his thinking and actions reveal his own respect for the earlier prophets, and his unique contribution to the Biblical momentum where people of faith confront systemic injustice in the empires they face.

It seems to me that if we respect the messages of the Old Testament, and strive to understand them in their authentic context, then we may actually discover a deeper harmony in the entire sweep of scripture, which does not require us to take anything out of context. Without gerrymandering the scriptures, but simply in appreciating them, we may come to see that their message has an elegant consistency that needs no further embellishment. We may not need to look so hard for a connection between the story of Jesus and the stories of the Torah, the Law, and the Prophets. That connection may be right in front of our eyes if we see scripture through this lens of God and Empire that Crossan identifies.

The final reason why it is important for modern Christian audiences to study the Old Testament, in its own context, is that ours is an increasingly multicultural and multi-faith society. In our congregations, we are more often speaking to people who live in interfaith families in which one spouse has grown up as a Jew. Not only is it disrespectful to Judaism to read the Old Testament as nothing more than a prelude to the New Testament, it may be disrespectful to some of our listeners, and thwart the opportunity for more interfaith dialogue in our churches. To the extent that we can understand Jewish faith and scripture, we can build bridges, which is what many modern worshippers are seeking.

In recent years, other preachers and scholars have tried to address what they see as weaknesses in the *New Revised Common Lectionary.* Some share my concerns, and others have their own concerns.[4] A growing number of pastors have found ways to supplement the lectionary with a fourth year of readings. In his book *Beyond the Lectionary,* David Ackerman raises an important concern about the lectionary's limited number of Sunday readings, which only include twenty five percent of scripture. Ackerman adds a year's worth of readings in order to include some new stories that he believes are very preach-able. A pulpit veteran and homiletics teacher, his additional texts are original and his book offers some new perspectives to those committed to lectionary preaching, but who are interested in fresh options and new variety. Episcopal priest, John Butcher has created *An Uncommon Lectionary* by supplementing the standard gospel readings with readings from extra-canonical material from the gospel of Thomas, The

---

4. See Steven Thorngate's article in *Christian Century* for a full review of projects that question the lectionary and offer amendments to it, including supplementary or alternative sets of readings.

Gospel of Mary, and the Didache. Tom Bandy has created a lectionary for seekers and those who come to church with no religious background. Another prominent writer, Martha Simmons, has critiqued the *New Revised Common Lectionary* for being out of touch with worship patterns in most African American churches today. She has chaired a group of scholars who have created an African American Lectionary with its own liturgical calendar, designed for the unique needs and worship patterns in historically Black churches. Timothy Slemmons has published a fourth year of lections, called *Year* D, that provides additional selections from the Old Testament to address the imbalance in the lectionary's treatment of the Hebrew Bible.

In 2010, Craig Koester and Rolf Jacobson created a narrative lectionary with a four-year cycle aimed at demonstrating some of the overarching Biblical themes; they share their ideas at workshops and on their website. Koester believes that each year should be devoted to one of the gospels, and informed by the narrative theme of that gospel. While many of these authors raise many of the same concerns that I do, to my knowledge none have gone so far as to suggest a new system for preaching that sidesteps the lectionary completely. However, the emerging variety of alternatives points to a widening interest in re-thinking lectionary preaching, and points to a growing conversation about how to seek some new ways to preach.

4

Teach It

When a good preacher gets into a sermon in some exuberant worship services, you might hear an enthusiastic listener offer a word of encouragement by yelling out "preach it." I have never heard anyone yell, "teach it," but I would like to suggest that many people in our churches come hoping for a chance to learn about life from someone who is prepared to teach them.

When a new minister is ordained in the United Church of Christ, the ordination vows include a number of questions. One of those questions is, "Will you be faithful in preaching *and teaching* the gospel?" Most ministers are aware of their responsibility to preach, but many forget the responsibility to *teach*. Emphasizing the role of teaching the congregation is crucial, because preachers often underestimate the impact they can make when they take teaching as seriously as they take preaching. The kind of teaching we overlook is not the kind that we do in classes or Bible study, but the teaching done from the pulpit. Most church members look up to preachers as the authority on faith, and the prime instructor in religion. All good teachers take teaching seriously, and they know intuitively that, in order to really make a difference in the lives of their students, they need to know their audience. The relationship between shepherd and flock informs congregational worship, reminding the preacher that worship is, at its roots, a dialogue between God and the people, in which the preacher is the go-between, or the matchmaker. Keeping this model in mind, it is important to be aware of the resources that come from the lived experience of the congregation, and present themselves to the preacher.

Conversations with new members about what brought them to our church, and what they are seeking in a church, has always taught me a lot. Often new members recount a story about a child who asked a spiritual question that they could not answer. By the time they are four or five years old, many children enter a period of spiritual inquiry. It is not uncommon for them to ask all kinds of questions that push their parents into theological terrain. Some of these questions arise innocently enough; Where does God live? What happened to Grandpa when he died? Did our guinea pig go to heaven? Yet lots of parents do not feel confident that they are prepared for these discussions, and suddenly feel the need for religious resources. For many families with young children, one perplexing question about Jesus, or heaven, or death, can provoke a conversation in which the parents acknowledge that they need help.

One family told me that their four-year-old Emma was excited about Christmas, and, as the holiday approached, her mother took out the old family crèche. She told Emma the story of the birth of Jesus as she showed her the pieces of the nativity set, one by one. After arranging the shepherds, lambs, wise men, and the camel, they got to the manger. When it was time to put the baby in the manger, Emma looked at her mom and said, "I forgot the baby's name; it is Santa Claus, right?" That night Emma's parents looked at each other with a mixture of amusement and horror, and quickly agreed that it was time to find a church for their growing family.

Many other people come to church without the direct prompting of a child's question. A miraculous or difficult birth can deepen someone's outlook. The move to a new town can make competent people feel alone. Career changes, or difficult diagnoses, or a child's unexpected needs, can leave people feeling lost. Concerns about how to survive a divorce or deal with depression can jolt families onto a new quest for faith. For good or ill, life challenges and changes can rock even sturdy people to their foundations. They arrive with pastoral needs, but also with deeper questions of faith that they may not be able to articulate.

Whatever the initial motivation or presenting issue, many families come looking for help with life. They may arrive asking for Sunday School, but they may also be very grateful to learn about how to be faithful parents, or how to be emotionally re-silient, or how to be spiritually grounded. They may not seek to learn more about the Bible, but be pleasantly surprised to discover the Bible has good psychological insights into their relationships. Whether they ask for information or not, I believe that people come to church to learn things that they cannot find anywhere else. Perhaps, it seems obvious that the church and its leaders have a major responsibility to teach the congregation, but the minister's teaching role can often be overlooked. Clergy can lose sight of the fact that pastors enjoy a unique opportunity to impart a kind of wisdom that people cannot find at work, on television, or on the internet. It is too easy for the church to forget that it holds the key to a treasure trove of information that you cannot find in a search engine.

In a study of six-hundred-and-sixty-seven clergy in Chicago, it was discovered that administrative expectations often crowded out teaching expectations—a main cause in clergy burnout. Clergy, who chose the profession expecting to do preaching and teaching, discovered that they spent so much time in administration that it shifted what they could accomplish. Preaching could not be jet-tisoned, but teaching often suffered.[1]

In approaching this challenge, it can prove to be a mistake to compartmentalize families that seek Christian Education for their children. What most Protestant churches offer are children's education programs with a curriculum in faith basics, while fail-ing to recognize their responsibility to teach the adults the same

1. Hoge, et al. "Influence of Role," 3.

curriculum at their level. While it is easy to assume that Christian Education responsibilities are met by instructing the children and youth, when we neglect the spiritual formation needs of the adult population, we may undermine the spiritual development of their offspring, too. Any comparison between the amount of time children spend in Sunday school with the amount of time they spend with their parents the rest of the week, makes me wonder why churches fail to put a stronger emphasis on the faith development of the adults in the family.

The irony is that parents often seek a church because they feel inadequate to teach their children religion, but the church responds by directing its energy toward instructing the children, and not the parents, thus continuing to make the parents feel inadequate. If, instead, we affirm that all of us in the faith community, that is, preachers, parents, Sunday School teachers, confirmation mentors, youth group advisors, and other adults, hold a shared responsibility for teaching faith from a variety of perspectives, then we may have a more effective model for passing faith from one generation to the next. Children gain a great deal simply by belonging to a community where adults support one another on a shared faith pilgrimage. What the church can offer is never a substitute for the parents' influence, but we have a real role to play in supporting the natural teaching that occurs in all families as they pass on spiritual truth, wise counsel, and the tenets of religion, in one form or another. At its best, the church provides an environment that fosters teaching, and creates a space where children and adults engage in lively discussions about faith's questions and answers. It can offer books, music, and stories that share practical examples of how to talk about faith, thus enriching families by inviting them to be part of an informal village that nurtures the spiritual life of each generation.

In our baptism liturgy we ask the parents, "Will you promise to grow with this child in the faith?" I believe that this is a great question because it reminds us that children teach us, and that we all learn from one another, but it also reminds us that children often push us to the deep wells of self-understanding. Parents assume that the church will help them know how to teach their children, but the church holds up a new vision of little children leading us all, and the promise, at least in the Baptism liturgy, that new parents begin their own faith exploration because of these new little people in their lives. When people come to church to learn, whether it is through the prompting of their children or their own childlike curiosity, they acknowledge that secular education only goes so far in providing wisdom. Jewish custom is instructive here. Synagogues are all led by rabbis, and that title simply means "teacher." Using the title rabbi keeps the teaching function on the minds of the congregation at all times.

Tertullian wrote, "Christians are made [i.e.fashioned or formed], not born." Referring to Tertullian, John Westerhoff writes:

> God, I suggest will not judge either parents or the adults in the community on how the children turn out, but God will judge the adults in the church on how they turn out, and that is enough for us all to lose sleep over. The issue is not what we have done to or for our children in an attempt to make them turn out as we see fit, but what we have done faithfully with our children, in an attempt to influence their understanding and ways of life.[2]

Any curriculum for the children in a church will be rendered somewhat useless if it fails to be reinforced by an adult curriculum on faith, rooted in the Bible.

In his book *Traveling Together: A Guide for Disciple-Forming Congregations,* Jeffrey Jones writes, "Effective discipleship with children is only possible when effective discipleship with adults is happening. We cannot help children grow as disciples unless we ourselves are growing disciples."[3] Jones points to data demonstrating that whether they grew up in a church or not, adults today are spiritually hungry, though they may be uncertain about what they seek, or skeptical that churches can meet these needs. Unfulfilling childhood experiences in a church, combined with bad press that the Christian churches have garnered of late, have made it difficult

2. Westerhoff, *Will Our Children,* 134.

3. Jones, *Traveling,* 67.

for the general public to distinguish between Christian denominations, and therefore, easy to be wary of all churches. Although many of these poorly churched, or unchurched, men and women arrive looking for help teaching their children religion, most of them respond favorably when churches provide both instruction for the children and faith resources for the whole family.

One of the basic ways that ministers teach people about the faith is through the weekly sermon. Often we think that the audience for this message is primarily the adults of the congregation, but, in this chapter, I have also tried to establish that there may be ripple effects that prove beneficial to entire families. Preachers hold the audience's attention for the central segment of every worship service, a surprisingly long period of time in a world of sound-bytes. Preachers have the chance each week to show people the rich resources of scripture, and to demonstrate the ways that the Bible holds timeless truth that is perpetually current and pertinent to life as we know it. But preachers also have the chance to connect the Bible stories with modern psychology, politics, history, current events, and contemporary issues.

Whether we gave it much thought or not, over the years I imagine that many pastors who have used *the New Revised Common Lectionary* have assumed that all that was necessary to teach the congregation was to prepare effective sermons on the texts assigned by the lectionary. We tacitly trusted that the suggested readings would offer an adequate faith curriculum. While it may not have been stated explicitly, the assumption for many preachers was that their job was completed if they addressed the topics raised by the scripture lessons suggested in the lectionary. Hence, those who preached from it would automatically cover all of the pedagogical bases.

Indeed, as I have suggested, the lectionary has its own educational framework and teaching goals, and they are all based on the Christian calendar. The lectionary assumes that by experiencing Jesus' birth, life, death, and resurrection in liturgy and sermons, the church learns essential doctrine and finds sufficient instruction in the faith, primarily from the way that the church reenacts these moments in sacred time and space. The theory for those who use the lectionary is that worshippers will attend services regularly, appreciate the theological rationale behind the lectionary, and find the time to become educated about it. I leave it to others to speculate about whether worship attendance was ever sufficiently consistent, or intellectual curiosity compelling enough, to make the lectionary an effective curriculum, but I would argue that today's uneven worship attendance might be enough to make one question its suitability as an adequate faith curriculum.One of the pioneers in thematic preaching is Marlin Lavanhar, Senior Minister of All Souls Unitarian Universalist Church in Tulsa, Oklahoma. Arriving at All Souls in 2000, Lavanhar decided the adults in his congregation were not receiving adequate instruction in the Unitarian Universalist tradition, and designed a three-year curriculum that established monthly themes for three consecutive program years. "When I was in my first year of ministry here I realized I needed something with a little more structure," [Lavanhar] says. "UU ministers have to work a little harder to come up with sermon topics because, for the most part, we don't follow the lectionary that traditional Christian ministers do." There is a more significant reason for using monthly themes than just the need to be better organized, he notes. "I want our members to have a systematic theology. There are certain core topics that people need to know about to have a good core grounding in liberal theology."[4] In his teaching role, Lavanhar designed his own pulpit curriculum, though he did not call it that. His monthly themes were based on implicit teaching goals.

Starting in 2002, All Souls created a curriculum for the entire church, with programs for adults and children, all guided by these monthly themes. The curriculum is deliberately general and theologically broad, so that the topics allow room for creativity. Listed below are the topics used at All Souls; they rotate through a three-year pattern.

4. Chalice World, "Monthly Themes."

Year One	Year Two	Year Three
Forgiveness	Unity	Vision
Death	Vocation	Creation
Faith	Gratitude	Democracy
Hope	Peace	God
Justice	Grace	Authority
Love	Prayer	Evil
Brokenness	Letting go	Redemption
Transformation	Salvation	Freedom
Transcendence	Truth	Mercy

While different churches and denominations would put together their own themes that reflect their unique theological lenses, this template offers suggestions that have been used successfully. To my mind, these topics are not specific to the Unitarian Universalist setting, and offer general themes of religious inquiry that would be of interest to a broad range of churches. What All Souls has done is identify the kinds of salient issues that a theological curriculum should address, whether it will be used in a Unitarian Universalist setting or some other one. Lavanhar's experience demonstrates that preachers can design a pulpit curriculum more easily if they approach the preaching schedule with an idea of what they want to convey, and design a set of core questions.

The trip to Tulsa gave me a lot to consider, and I admired Lavanar's way of organizing his sermon themes around the basic principles of a Unitarian Universalist curriculum. After my trip to Tulsa, I gave thought to what a curriculum might look like in my own church. What topics would it include? What would be its guiding principles? If the *New Revised Common Lectionary* was organized around the theme of the Incarnation, what were some other principles that might serve to form the basis of a new curriculum? Could I build a curriculum around the notion of covenant, or hope? Even for people steeped in the Bible, the number of possibilities was staggering.

As I considered these questions, I realized that any good curriculum involves a negotiation between what the teacher hopes to convey, and what the people ask for. In my early years as a preacher, the pendulum often tilted to what I hoped to impart, but in later years I have learned that preaching is a humbling business. It has often taught me to recognize that the best resource for sermons was right in front of me—the people in the pews. The better sermons don't rely on expertise, but rather on the ability to answer the questions that the people are really asking. Some of the sermons I considered most enlightened did not seem to touch the people in my pews, and some of the messages that I thought were overly basic proved to hit the mark in ways I never expected, because they connected with people. It would be hard to underestimate the importance of this consideration for pastors and preachers over the centuries. It reminds us of the symbiotic relationship between the pulpit and the pew. The best preaching is not the delivery of a masterpiece, but the ability to engage in an ongoing public conversation about faith. This positions the preacher as less of an expert, and more of the facilitator of a dialogue in which the preacher has a stake in the conversation too. Preachers are often surprised by their reliance on their people, but it is a lesson that is learned and relearned throughout the course of ministry.

There is an old story about John Wesley that illustrates this truth. The founder of Methodism was starting his ministry in 1738 when he grew confused and sought advice from his mentor, a Moravian missionary, Peter Bohler. Apparently, Wesley found his sense of personal mission solidified when he felt his "heart strangely warmed" at the Alder's Gate in London, but before Wesley had that spiritual awakening he was unsure about his faith, and he grew discouraged about how to preach about salvation because he was, himself, so skeptical. Exhausted over time, he reasoned that he could not preach to others if he lacked his own conviction. Wesley asked Bohler if he should stop preaching, but Bohler replied, "By no means." Wesley wondered, "But what can I preach?" Bohler replied, "Preach faith until you have it, and then when you have it, you will preach faith."[5] Wesley took Bohler's advice, and it marked a turning point for him. Like most of us, Wesley started with the

5. Telford, *John Wesley,* Chapter 7.

impression that he was solely responsible for conveying faith to his flock. And so he considered leaving the ministry because he did not possess enough faith to share substantially every week. When his early mentor suggested that he preach faith until he found it himself, he reminded him that, in meeting the needs of his congregation, his own needs would be met, and his consecration would deepen too. Pastor-parish relationships are symbiotic relationships in which the questions of faith propel all parties into dialogue. As a preacher responds to the issues of life and the questions these issues raise, his or her own faith matures and is strengthened too.

A lot rides on the sermon. While oratory was common throughout thousands of years of world history, the sermon is one of the few modern examples of a time when adults gather to listen to someone speak. Given how rare it is today for people to listen to one voice speaking without much other distraction, modern preachers have great incentive to get their message right. Because of this, the sermon needs to answer the questions people are asking, and address the topics they really care about. What are people seeking to know when they come to church today? To understand what the flock is truly seeking, pastors may need to listen not only to what people say, but also dig down to try to discern what people really mean. In listening closely to the questions people ask, and to the deeper messages within those questions, pastors can address the things people may never articulate but truly seek to know. Here is a sampling of the questions that I have heard people asking, in one way or another.

- How do I find purpose in my life?
- How do I grow in faith?
- How do I find happiness?
- Who was Jesus and what difference does his life make to mine?
- Does God listen to us? How should we pray?
- How do I forgive or find forgiveness?

- How do we live with faith in a multi-cultural world?
- Does the Bible support my modern values?

This exercise of listening to people's questions of faith reminds me of what Rick Warren did in Orange County. When he was trying to start a new church there in the early nineties, he took eighteen months to conduct interviews with people who lived in the area. At the time it was thought to be a lot of upfront market research, but the interviews allowed him to get to know the audience he was hoping to attract. One lesson from the success of the Saddleback Church is that the listening he did really paid off. The other lesson in Warren's story is much more subtle. He had the gift of knowing how to listen, so he really heard what they were saying, and perceived how far they could be coaxed to go. He realized that they did not like organ music, but would sit through a pretty long sermon. In my church, when I had the group of families with adults who needed to be baptized, I was initially baffled about why they remained unwilling to join the church. It took a certain level of persistence and listening to discover their concerns about baptism, and then to talk about baptism with them in a way that made sense so we could find a way to go forward together.

As I listened to the questions that people were asking, and then drilled down to the under-lying questions in some cases, I began to seek ways to address those issues in sermons. Unlike the UU's, in our church the Bible is the springboard for every message about faith, and I began to look for topics in scripture that would answer the contemporary questions of faith that I was hearing in conversations with parishioners. In this way I began to put together the rudiments of a Protestant pulpit curriculum. It took form through trial and error as I wrestled with the questions I hoped to answer.

How do I find purpose in life?

In answer to this question I preached a series of sermons on Christian vocation. This topic served as an effective way to remind people that God often calls us to new paths in our careers, in our devotional lives, and in service to others. The examples of biblical characters who heard a call to embark on a journey of faith and self-discovery can be found throughout the Bible; indeed, the theme of vocation is one of the most prevalent topics in both the Old and New Testaments. Examples of people who heard God's call include Abraham, Moses, Samuel, Esther, Peter, and Paul. Sermons about these Bible characters explore their experiences, and serve to normalize the notion and prospect of God's call. This well established biblical pattern reminds us that God habitually reaches out to people, and the variety of characters who respond to his call conveys the understanding that anyone might be called upon to chart a new path, or to build a deeper relationship with God.

How can I grow in faith?

I addressed this question with a series of sermons on the stages of faith, establishing the idea that faith is a journey, and throughout our lives we grow in a deeper understanding of God. One example of teaching from the pulpit is a sermon series that explores Moses' life as a pattern for the stages of faith formation. Step one is hearing God's call by "cultivating curiosity," as Moses did at the burning bush. Step two is "confronting fear," as Moses did when he faced Pharaoh. Step three is "taking action," as Moses did when he crossed the Red Sea. Step four is "perseverance," as Moses showed when he led the people for four decades. Step five is "finding the promised land," which the Hebrews demonstrated when they experienced transformation, and settled in a new region. Although there is a formulaic quality to this sermon series, I have discovered it offers some handles for faith that listeners can grasp and hold onto easily.

Similar series can be developed using the lives of Jacob and Paul. Using Jacob's story, a series might include sermons about his call in a dream, his maturity, his life with Laban, his return to Esau, and his wrestling with God. The theme of wrestling as a path to growth might connect the whole series. Paul's life also lends itself to a sermon series on spiritual growth, with sermons on his vision and baptism, his conversion, and his missions. This series might be contained within the overarching theme of vision.

How do I find happiness?

One could make the case that the whole of biblical literature is a treatise on how to find happiness. A series of sermons on the Ten Commandments, the beatitudes, or the parables can offer fundamental advice about how to find wholeness and deep satisfaction in life. Sermons that discuss how to be content, how to find wisdom, how to avoid temptation, and how to be whole, address questions that many contemporary seekers are interested in. One of our most popular sermon series came as a surprise. It was a series about good and evil, based on the seven deadly sins. I discovered that this series on the seven deadly sins was popular with modern audiences because it focused attention on how one finds real satisfaction in a secular and materialistic world. This theme proved to be both timeless and timely.

Who was Jesus and what difference does his life make in mine?

This question provides the opportunity to explore the meaning of Jesus' life, and why he matters today. It may provide the chance to tease out old assumptions, pat answers, and unfulfilling platitudes about Jesus. One approach has been to study Jesus from a different perspective each week: rabbi/teacher, healer, revolutionary, and man of peace. Another series on Jesus might include profiles of Jesus as subversive, savior, suffering servant, or mystic. One can make strong cases for each perspective, and exploring them weekly fleshes Jesus out in all his complexity. Like the story of the blind men with the elephant, this kind of series provides the opportunity to acknowledge the real variety of views about the man at the center of the Christian faith. Any church that takes discipleship seriously needs to reexamine Jesus in a basic and thorough way, with some regularity.

Does God listen to us? How should we pray?

Like the original disciples who asked Jesus to teach them to pray, contemporary men and women also yearn for advice about speaking to God. The Lord's Prayer is both an example of devotion, and a primer on starting a conversation with God. This prayer continues to fascinate people of faith. A series that explains and unpacks the prayer, line by line, addresses the modern seeker's question about learning to pray. The prayer itself teaches lessons about God's authority ("hallowed be thy name"), God's vision ("thy kingdom come"), God's providence ("give us this day our daily bread"), God's wisdom ("forgive us our debts as we forgive our debtors"), and God's perpetual guidance ("lead us not into temptation but deliver us from evil"). It also demonstrates how to develop a prayerful attitude toward God.

How do I forgive, or find forgiveness?

This question is one that weighs heavily on many people's minds. A series of sermons on various challenges of forgiveness can begin to quench the thirst for guidance in this area. For example, the series might address the following questions: How do I forgive my family? How do I forgive my spouse? How do I forgive myself? How do I forgive God? Stories like Jacob and Esau, or Joseph and his brothers, raise many questions about forgiving your family. Stories about Isaac and Rebecca, or Sarah and Abraham, raise questions about how to forgive a spouse. Peter's denial of Jesus highlights the issue of forgiving yourself. The story of Job is an obvious choice as a text for a sermon on forgiving God.

How do we live with faith in a multicultural world?

In answering this question, I preached a series about "boundaries." The Bible has many examples of boundary crossing in both testaments. The stories are everywhere: Ruth and Rahab, The Samaritan Woman and the Good Samaritan, both Josephs (the one with the coat and the one with the baby) are boundary crossers. Paul's conversion, Phillip and the Ethiopian Eunuch, and Peter and Cornelius all offer examples of multi-cultural stories. This sermon series turned out to be a surprise because I did not expect to find so many relevant biblical examples of people who explore a question I had assumed was thoroughly modern. A sermon series on this topic can include sermons on justice, as well as interfaith dialogue. In our church the topic sparked lively conversations and responses. (More ideas for sermons on the "neighbor" topic appear in Appendix B.)

Does the Bible really support my modern values?

Many sermons answer this question implicitly every week, but sometimes it is good to offer an explicit approach to the topic. Families of all ages may be delighted to discover that the Bible has relevant resources for them, and that fundamentalists do not hold the only keys to the biblical interpretation of family values. In our series, we addressed the stress on nuclear families, the importance of community, how generations learn from one another, communication skills, honesty, and building character. We also addressed this question in another sermon series on love; one sermon talked about gay marriage, another sermon discussed unrequited love, and the last one looked at how to show respect in inter-faith communities.

It came as a surprise to many worshippers to find so many Bible stories with modern treatments of jealousy, infidelity, homicide, greed, lust, and general bad behavior. It was refreshing to learn that the Bible was not uniform in its messages about how to handle thorny family issues. The sermon series—What Does the

Bible Really Say about Family Values?—offered us the chance to consider family values as a much more complex subject with fewer black-and-white prescriptions than most people had assumed.

A PULPIT CURRICULUM

What kinds of resources do preachers need to put together sermons that address these kinds of questions? Along with my own realization that the lectionary was not a complete curriculum for my congregation, came a growing concern that I needed to be more conscientious about my own preaching curriculum. I realized that whether I stated it, explicitly or not, I was always imparting some curriculum in the preaching texts I chose. There was an implicit slant created by the stories I included or omitted, the emphasis I placed on certain parts of the Bible, and how I explained theology. This led me to develop a basic list of questions that I believe a preacher should address from the pulpit. Any preacher might create his or her own set of questions before outlining teaching goals for a year of sermons. Here are mine:

- What are the foundational stories of Judaism and Christianity?
- Who are the important Biblical heroes and characters? What do we learn from their stories?
- What is the Biblical understanding of covenant?
- What is the story of the birth of Jesus, and what does it mean?
- What are the teachings of Jesus?
- What is the meaning of Jesus' death and resurrection?
- How did the early church begin?
- What is the meaning of the creeds?
- What is the significance of the church's rites and sacraments?
- What does the Judeo-Christian faith say to us about how to put our faith into action?

Within these topics I have identified some concepts that I believe are essential to understanding the sweep of scripture and the underpinnings of our faith. The list includes some broad fundamental goals as well as practical ways to apply faith. A set of questions about how to practice faith, combined with the goals for a pulpit curriculum, offers the foundation for planning a year of sermons. This is an ambitious list of topics. However, with these questions as a backdrop for the preaching menu, the goals become a compass to navigate the sea of scripture in search of texts. Identifying the questions is the hardest part of this exercise. Once the teaching goals have been established, they quickly inform sermon preparation and program development. A good pulpit curriculum comes from a negotiation between theological and pastoral questions.

In Appendix C, I offer a list of texts that I propose as a biblical curriculum for preaching, or Pulpit Curriculum. It is a selection of good Bible stories for sermons that form the framework for a solid Christian understanding of biblical faith. I hope to at least mention all of these stories in a three-year preaching cycle. In designing this curriculum, I assumed that most church members receive the majority of their faith instruction from listening to sermons. There is nothing unique about my curriculum, and it would be a wonderful exercise for any preacher to design one, or to challenge some church leaders or students of the Bible to develop their own curriculum. It is meant to accompany, and to supplement, the three-year cycle of sermon topics that I will introduce in chapter 6. In that chapter, I will demonstrate how to use the scripture lessons listed in the curriculum in various sermon series to illustrate the preaching themes.

Preachers who appreciate the role of rabbi, or primary educator, and choose sermon topics with an eye toward leveraging that role, can increase their impact. It is often the people in the pews who remind me of what they are searching for. To my surprise, a sermon on forgiveness brings someone in for pastoral advice. A sermon on prayer might provoke someone to ask for a spiritual retreat. A sermon on grief might strike a deep chord, and provide the catalyst for a support group.

One of the best contemporary examples of a religious leader who has embraced this teaching role wholeheartedly is Harold Kushner, Rabbi Emeritus of Temple Israel in Natick, Massachusetts. Best known for his book on grief, in which he publicly explored the loss of his own son, Kushner also wrote *When Children Ask about God: A Guide for Parents Who Don't Always Have All the Answers.* This book, from earlier in his career, reveals how he saw his role as someone who spent his life turning pastoral questions into teachable moments. He shared the faith he found in the Bible in books like *Who Needs God? How Good do We Have To Be?, Living a Life that Matters,* and *When All You Ever Wanted Isn't Enough.* By applying the Bible's wisdom to everyday issues, Kushner's books have reached Jews and Christians, and have succeeded in feeding a deep hunger in many people from all faiths. By addressing contemporary questions of faith, like doubt, disappointment, the nature of God, and unanswered prayer, Kushner has become a teacher not only for people who rely on Jewish wisdom, but for people from many faith traditions. His success at reaching a crossover audience from other religions, and none at all, has only served to prove that many men and women are eagerly searching for this kind of religious teaching.

5

Finding Preaching Themes in Scripture

I RECOGNIZE THAT PREACHING with themes will require a new approach to exegesis and sermon preparation. It is one thing to critique some of the weaknesses in the *New Revised Common Lectionary,* and quite another to propose a whole new system for organizing weekly sermons. For most preachers who have grown accustomed to lectionary preaching, it is no small departure to adopt this new approach, and I don't want to underestimate the significance of this shift. But, I would like to demonstrate that biblical themes are easy to spot when you begin to search for them, and I hope to show in this chapter that scripture lends itself to preaching with themes. I have outlined some themes that run through both testaments. By identifying some examples of biblical themes, I hope to show how quickly preachers can reorient sermon preparation time, and discover a new way of finding sermon texts.

As I developed this new approach to preaching, it required that I begin to look at scripture differently. When I was depending exclusively on the lectionary, I began with a set of readings each week from which to choose sermon texts, but when I decided to change to preaching with themes, suddenly I found it was necessary to choose preaching texts in a whole new way. Instead of starting with an assigned passage and then trying to explain it and illustrate it, I started with a topic and then searched through scripture for examples of how the Bible addressed the topic. This shift completely reversed the exegetical process for my sermon preparation. At first, I found there were some challenges, but then I discovered that the new approach also freed me to preach more creatively. I felt as though I had been released to search through scripture to find my own path. It also provided a chance to read the Bible without the biases that I had identified in the lectionary.

While the Bible defies attempts to contain it within a handful of simple topics, it does offer some thematic motifs that are developed consistently throughout the stories of faith. These narratives are rich and multifaceted. The truths running through them are complex, varied, and by no means simplistic, but many of the messages are repeated or explored in a variety of settings. In the sections that follow, I have identified some preaching themes that run through the stories in both the Old and New Testaments. Far from exhaustive, this list of themes is merely suggestive of the kinds of topics that lend themselves to thematic preaching, and could be developed easily into a series of sermons that address contemporary questions of faith.

THEME ONE: GOD'S COMMITMENT

Sermons often stress our human dependence on God, but Holy Scripture is also replete with examples, sometimes more subtly developed, of God's commitment to human beings, and furthermore, of God's vulnerability in this covenant relationship. God's commitment to the relationship is tried and tested in some of the oldest stories in the Bible, and God's love is often demonstrated most dramatically in times of testing.

Adam and Eve

Few stories in the Bible have been analyzed more than the story of creation, which begins in Gen 2. While many theologians point to this episode as the prime explanation for original sin, one can also make an equally strong case for the way it demonstrates growth and change. Where some see the destruction of an ideal and once-perfect world, others find a relationship between God and people that shifts and deepens. It changes as God experiences betrayal and anger, and as the people live with remorse and a loss of innocence. What is ultimately interesting and telling here is that God does not destroy Adam and Eve, which was always an option. The second story of creation provides a very poetic description of the negotiation inevitable as children outgrow the gardens of youth. Two details support this interpretation, and demonstrate a kindness at the heart of God's nature. Both are recounted in Gen 3.

The first takes place when God confronts the couple after they have eaten the fruit of the tree. Not unlike a human parent who confronts disobedient offspring, God has choices about how to handle this situation. Those choices have implications for the lessons that are taught. In this case, God already knows, or at least suspects, what has happened. So God might have confronted the couple (Gen 3:9–13) by accusing them of eating the forbidden fruit. God might have banished Adam and Eve on the spot, without explanation, forcing them to discover their mistake while subjected to the punishment of God's withdrawal into silence. God might have indulged in a tantrum, and lectured Adam and Eve about their mistakes. God might have exercised any number of harsh prerogatives.

Instead, God pursues Adam and Eve. They hide, and God tries to find them. God treats them as those who are lost, not like those who are fatally flawed. God engages them in conversation, and God's questions lead Adam and Eve to recognize their mistake. Where are you? Who told you that you were naked? What is this that you have done? With a remarkable openness, God challenges the people to consider what has happened in a manner that is not dismissive.

Then there is a final moment in this story, which reveals tenderness in God's affection that is not usually associated with the story of Adam and Eve. Following six verses that explain the consequences of this situation, one surprising detail changes everything. After banishing Adam and Eve from the Garden of Eden, "the Lord God made garments of skin for the man and for his wife, and clothed them" (Gen 3:21). Reminiscent of human parents who have given vent to their anger and disappointment, and then suddenly grab their children and hug them in a way that belies their wrath or explains it, God seals his love with an unexpected tenderness that is key to what they share.

In much the same way, this detail about God's tailoring efforts describes someone who may yell all afternoon, but who also sits up all night by the lamp, sewing clothes to keep his children warm and shielded from embarrassment. This is not the gesture of a God who is essentially unforgiving. Neither is this a God who has ceased to care, but rather one who has discovered that these creatures cannot be contained. In that one moment, God makes it clear that wherever they travel on this earth, they will be cared for. While there are consequences to their actions, God's gesture is less about banishing them than it is about releasing them into adulthood. Yet, even as they depart, God sends them off with handmade clothing, a visceral reminder of God's affection that they could feel on their backs every day. This story sets the tone and standard for God's commitment to humankind, but it is not unique in the way it illustrates God's compassion and connection to the people in the Bible.

Moses' Relationship

In Exodus 33 we learn about the relationship that Moses develops with God. Though he is the major figure in the Old Testament, Moses' humanity is central to his story. The story demonstrates his curiosity and bravery, as well as his fear and frustration. Exodus paints the portrait of a complex man of many emotions, which makes Moses accessible as a character, and suggests that the connection Moses has with God is not unique, but illustrative of the kind of relationship all people can cultivate with God. The Bible recounts the way that God would meet with Moses in the tent outside the camp. "The Lord used to speak to Moses face-to-face like two people talking to each other" (Exod 33:11, *Common English Bible* translation). The *New Revised Standard Version* supports this image: "The Lord used to speak to Moses face-to-face like one speaks to a friend."

The mention of Joshua, Moses' lieutenant, standing nearby (Exod 33:11), serves two purposes: first, it demonstrates that Moses has removed himself from the community; second, it provides details that normalize the event, and ground it in time and space. Moses meets with God, but his assistant Joshua is within earshot, implying that such connections *are* within the realm of our human experience. God may be off at a distance, but not separated from the rest of the people, including the readers.

The relationship between Moses and God is marked by openness and easy communication. Moses feels confident enough to confide in God and seeks a closer connection to God (Exod 33:18), even pushing the boundaries of their relationship. When Moses requests to see more of God, the Bible describes an enormous trust developing between God and humankind. Moses' request to see God speaks to a deep longing in many people. There is an aspect of the request that involves a hope to exert some control over God, but it also represents a desire to know God more fully than earth's bounds allow. God's response demonstrates that this relationship has both real intimacy, and real boundaries.

Hosea

One poetic example of the connection between God and the people comes from the minor prophet, Hosea. Set in the Northern Kingdom of Israel more than seven hundred years BCE, Hosea speaks at a time when Israel and Syria were fighting with Judah to force the southern kingdom to join the northern one in an alliance against the Assyrians. Hosea was a prophet in a time of religious pluralism, and he depicts Israel as a faithless wife, and God as an aggrieved husband; he also paints a picture of God as doting parent. This image reveals the softer side of God, and explains God's deep sense of betrayal.

> When Israel was a child I loved him and out of Egypt I called my son. The more I called the more they went from me . . . yet it was I who taught Ephraim to walk. I took them up in my arms but they did not know that I healed them. I led them with cords of human kindness, with bands of love. I was to them like those who lift infants to their cheeks. I bent down to them and fed them. (Hos 11:1–4)

Here God seems to be hovering over the young nation, fearful she will lose her footing and fall. Like a protective parent with a toddler, God's heart is fed by the smell of Israel's skin and the feel of Israel's cheeks. The metaphor helps to explain God's sense of betrayal when the Hebrews worshipped other gods.

Jesus' Crucifixion and Resurrection

All of the gospel accounts of the life and death of Jesus point ultimately to God's bedrock commitment to the human race. God's willingness to send a son so fearless and reckless, and yet so full of grace and truth, into the dangerous world of Galilee, under the Roman Empire, demonstrates God's ultimate commitment. John sums up this truth: "God so loved the world that he gave his only begotten son" (John 3:16), and exercised the enormous restraint required in allowing the world to reject him. God's commitment is most graphically illustrated in the event of the resurrection. No one would have blamed God for rescuing Jesus and then turning a blind eye on the fate of humanity, but God allowed Jesus to suffer and then accomplished the resurrection, that we might all know that this human enterprise is a hopeful journey because God has no intention of abandoning humankind.

THEME TWO: PRAYER IS A RESOURCE

Moses and the People

Three days after crossing the Red Sea, the Hebrews cannot find water to drink and they complain to Moses, who asks God for help. God responds by changing stagnant water into sweet water, and leading them to a place where many springs converge in the desert (Exod 15:22–27). Thus begins the conversation between God and the people. When they ask for food, God sends manna—an edible fungus which reminds them of bread. When they complain about the manna, God sends flocks of quail for meat every evening (Exod 16:1–8). This way, the Hebrews learn to rely on God's providence, and to trust that God will respond when they ask for help.

Jesus' Lessons

In the gospel of Luke, when the disciples ask Jesus to teach them to pray, he demonstrates how to talk to God in words we call "The Lord's Prayer." Jesus begins the prayer using the word "Abba" (Matt 6:9), in Aramaic, an unprecedented familiarity for Jews, but one that connotes great intimacy. Jesus conveys such trust in God that he teaches his disciples they can trust God with their petitions and their questions. With stories like the Parable of the Lost coin and the Prodigal Son in Luke, Jesus illustrates that God will seek them when they are wandering or lost.

Prayerful Intuition

Many people in the Old and New Testaments hear God's voice at key times in their lives. Here are three examples:

Samuel

When Samuel is selecting a king for Israel, the prophet goes to Bethlehem to choose someone to succeed King Saul from among the sons of Jesse. The young men stand in a line before Samuel, who approaches the eldest—a man whose stature and confidence convey his natural authority and aptitude for leadership. The prophet hears the voice of God in his head cautioning him. God says "Do not look on his appearance or on the height of his stature, because I have rejected him, for the Lord does not see as mortals see; they look on the outward appearance, but the Lord looks on the heart" (I Sam 16:6–7). Here we see the strong prayerful connection that enables Samuel to gain a sense of holy discernment, and he experiences it as though God were whispering in his ear.

Elijah

When Elijah challenges the prophets of Jezebel to a standoff, their magic is no match for Elijah's power, and the test results in a rout, where Elijah kills all the prophets of Baal. Jezebel is so angry that she threatens to kill Elijah in return, so the prophet takes his life in his hands and runs into the desert without provisions. Eventually he arrives in a cave where he hears God asking him why he has gone so far away. As Elijah confesses his fears, he is sustained by a conversation with God, and recognizes that God is his champion, and will search for him, pursuing him when he is lost, and protecting him when he is afraid. Throughout his life, Elijah is sustained by his ability to hear God's voice and feel God's presence when he is scared.

Peter and Cornelius

In Acts 10 there is a story about Peter and a centurion named Cornelius. Both men have visions in which they believe God is instructing them to meet. Peter is especially confused by this experience because he does not mingle with Gentiles. Though both men are puzzled by the messages they receive, their faith in their experience of reliably hearing God's voice gives them the courage to respond to these visions and seek one another out.

THEME THREE: HOSPITALITY

Sarah and Abraham

One day when Abraham is resting in his tent in the heat of the day, he looks up to see three strangers approaching the tent (Gen 18:6). Abraham invites them in and washes their feet. Then he instructs his wife, Sarah, to make fresh bread for them from choice flour, and instructs the servant to kill a calf so they might offer the best meat to their guests. These guests happen to be messengers from God, and this story demonstrates the way that people of faith are meant to greet strangers, as though they come with good news from God's own hand.

Jubilee Justice

Leviticus 25 declares that no one can take another's land indefinitely. One might have a string of bad crops, and need to pay debts by offering the family land in payment to creditors. But, people are forbidden from keeping another family's land for more than forty-nine years. That forty-ninth year was the year of Jubilee, when all debts were forgiven and all land was returned to the families that originally owned it. The Jubilee year reminds us that faith has always been forged in communities where people's fortunes might be unequal, but people are committed to care for each other over time. Hebrews harvesting the wheat are expected to leave some for the poor to glean in the fields. No one could claim to be faithful who ignored the least among them. A spirit of justice undergirds life in Israel, as all people wrestle with the challenge of what it means to love their neighbor as they love themselves.

Jesus

With a bold and even unorthodox view of human community, Jesus envisions a world where all people are treated as children of God. He demonstrates his radical inclusion by listening when lepers call for help, inviting tax collectors and prostitutes to dinner, talking openly to women, and inviting children into his circle. Seemingly blind to class, nationality, or race, Jesus responds to a centurion who is worried about his dying daughter (Matt 8:5–13 and Luke 7:2–10), and comforts an outcast Samaritan woman at a well (John 4:3–21). Shocking people on all sides, Jesus demonstrates a radical form of hospitality.

Philip and the Eunuch

When the apostle Philip meets an official from the court of the Ethiopian queen (Acts 8:26–40), Philip is uncertain about whether to have contact with this man who comes from a different race and nation. As the supervisor of the harem of a foreign queen, this castrated male would have been someone most Jews would be quick to avoid. But the Eunuch asks Philip to join him in Bible study, and invites the apostle into his chariot. In this moment, Philip decides to ignore the Jewish prohibitions about mingling with the man and responds with an open mind and heart. By the end of their visit, Philip baptizes the stranger, demonstrating the vision that the church is intended to be a place of inclusion, not exclusion.

THEME FOUR: FREEDOM

Exodus

The formative story of the Hebrew people is a saga about people who are sacrificing their lives to seek, and find, their freedom. The whole story of their political existence is about gaining freedom and keeping it. Once they settle in Canaan, the faith of their theocracy is based on an interpretation of how God responds to their efforts to maintain the safety of their borders. They see God's favor in times of political independence, and see God's punishment in periods of military and economic oppression. Freedom is the promise that creates this people, and pursuing their freedom is at the heart of who they are.

Jesus

Though he lives in a country that is controlled by the Roman Empire, and occupied by foreign soldiers, Jesus enjoys, and seems to relish, a remarkable degree of personal liberty. He speaks his mind, even when his words contain implied or thinly veiled threats to Roman rule. He toys with Roman customs, especially social rules of meal etiquette that fly in the face of standard convention. He sews seeds of unrest, challenging assumptions about class and gender. He confronts the Roman desire for order by publicly demonstrating his own lack of compliance. The greatest mark of his freedom is that he refuses to censor himself, no matter whom he offends. At his first appearance in his home synagogue, he almost loses his life when he enrages his audience by asserting that he is the one Isaiah foretold (Luke 4:29). Jesus lives with a radical freedom which Robin Meyers describes: "What is meant here by 'radical freedom' is not the shedding of all social or personal responsibilities or living a life of reckless abandon . . . It is a life lived outside of the straightjacket of fear and anxiety that controls most of us . . . What is missing is the despair that Soren Kierkegaard called the 'sickness unto death', that gnawing *angst* that shadows all our days . . . We are finite, vain and consumed with the fear that if we do not stay busy micromanaging the chaos of life, it will overwhelm us."[1]

Paul in Jail

The story of Paul and Silas' imprisonment (Acts 16:16–34) indicates that Paul has found such a freedom of spirit that his sense

1. Meyers, *Saving Jesus,* 50.

of his mission cannot be contained, even when he is in jail. One telling point in this story illustrates Paul's autonomy. There is an earthquake in the jail and the prisoners' chains are broken, and the jailer prepares to kill himself because he expects to be held responsible for the prisoners. But Paul prevents his jailer from doing himself harm, and reassures the man that he will not escape, even though he could. In the end, Paul demonstrates such freedom of mind and spirit that, while in this jail, he baptizes his jailer. Though incarcerated, Paul acts like a free man, refusing to treat his jailer as an enemy. No prison cell can dehumanize Paul, or thwart his mission to bring the message of Jesus to the world.

THEME FIVE: SPIRITUAL JOURNEY

Depictions of excursions in the Bible are often symbols of faith development. As it does in the Greek story *The Odyssey*, the motif of travel to new regions serves as a plot device to demonstrate character development and spiritual growth. When God calls Abraham to faith, the patriarch takes a trip. When Jacob leaves for a new land, the journey sets the stage for Jacob's encounter with God in a dream. When Joseph is abducted and sold into slavery, his trip to Egypt forms the backdrop for his growth in character and faith. Even the Israelites' journey into Babylonian captivity provides the momentum to codify religious law, write down oral tradition, and develop the religion we know as Judaism.

Exodus

The Jewish concept of covenant emanates from God's journey with the rescued slaves in the Exodus story. This foundational Biblical story is more than a tale of human liberation; it is a story of faith formation, in which the episodes illustrate the stages of that faith. As Moses takes the people from slavery on a forty-year trek through the wilderness, the Bible offers a paradigm for the way all people mature in faith. Here, I outline one approach to the sermon series I described on "stages of faith" in chapter 4.

1. Call to faith. God catches Moses' attention with a burning bush, and it is there that the curious patriarch hears the summons to embark on a new life mission. The experience of hearing God's voice and recognizing a divine call is so profound that the very soil Moses stands on seems to be holy ground.

2. Responding to God's call. Moses confronts Pharaoh, and demands the release of his slaves during an ambitious building campaign. The second step in faith formation involves facing one's fears of change, in order to embark on a new path.

3. Journey in faith. Moses leads the people into a desert where they learn to trust that God will feed them with manna each day. God gives Moses the Ten Commandments so that the people can learn to live together, travelling for forty years to acquire the lessons of freedom.

4. Wilderness. The journey includes times of doubt, frustration, and rebellion. The Hebrews discover that being confused and lost are part and parcel of the faith journey. The formative story of Judaism describes people who wander in circles for decades; yet the experience becomes emblematic of a time when God was near, and the Hebrews felt deeply connected to God. The Exodus reminds us that detours and apparent dead ends in life can include times of great spiritual awakening.

5. Promised Land. The Hebrew journey culminates when the people own a new identity and settle in a new land that is very different from Egypt. This story offers hope to all who would seek human transformation, and the fruits of religious pilgrimage.

The Exodus provides a faith curriculum, which lends itself to a sermon series. Framing this journey as the template for the various stages of faith is only one of many ways to use it.

Ruth

A Moabite woman inexplicably loyal to her mother-in-law, Ruth, decides to return to her dead husband's homeland; in the bargain, she abandons hope of reconnecting with her family, and risks a life of poverty. Yet her bold sense of adventure is unusual for her time and gender, making Ruth dependent on God's grace and guidance. This stubborn boundary-crossing anomaly of a woman catches God's attention, and that thrusts her into a new role as the bearer of God's blessing. She who refuses to be defined by her misfortune, and chooses instead to be known for her loyalty to a curious dream, is plucked from obscurity to become the wife of Boaz, and the great-grandmother of King David. Ruth's character informs the genetic mix of this future king. Ruth's determination to go where no one, not even Naomi, advises her to go makes her an example of someone willing to leave home, explore the world, and make of her life an adventure.

Jesus and Paul.

Jesus and Paul are also known for their nomadic ministries. Jesus refers to his life of travel when he says, "Foxes have dens and birds have nests but the Son of Man has nowhere to lay his head" (Luke 9:58). From the time Paul is called to Christianity, he seems to be on one mission after another, visiting churches, leaving them for new mission destinations, and then sending letters of encouragement back to the communities he has founded. His entire work is done while on the go. Many of the lessons of faith that we associate with Jesus also took place on the road: his parables, his healings, and his conversations with followers. For Jesus, these journeys serve as the backdrop for his emerging vision of the kingdom of

God. For Paul, his continuous movement informs his vision of the church he is so instrumental in creating.

THEME SIX: ABUNDANT LIFE

Creation

The first evidence of life's abundance is seen in Gen 1. A more circumspect view of life would not begin its holy text with such a lush description of the creation of the world. The very repetition in the language that recounts the sequences of God's creative endeavors points to the abundance that overlays and undergirds the earth. Both the detail and the repetition in this chapter describe God's abundant hand in the creation of the world.

Land of Milk and Honey

God calls the Hebrew slaves out of Egypt, but God calls them to something more than just a new existence; God promises them a land flowing with milk and honey. They are called not just to freedom, but to a wholly new and abundant experience of life. That vision of abundant life is a homeland where food and drink will be plentiful, and people will thrive. Personal fulfillment and deep contentment become their expectation. Moses promises them that God is leading them to a life which is so much more than survival, and people are destined to live in a place where food and drink flow in endless supply. The message is that we are destined to discover that life will exceed our expectations, and that our hard effort and perseverance will be rewarded in ways we cannot even imagine.

Wedding at Cana

In John's Gospel, Jesus is at a wedding in Cana when the wine runs out. Reluctantly, Jesus turns the water into wine. The surprise in this story is that the wine that is produced is much better quality than anyone expected. The miracle does more than address the scarcity of wine; it provides a new wine that raises the standards of refreshment (John 2:1-10).

Loaves and Fish

When Jesus offers thanks for the lunch of a little boy (John 6:1-14), the meal is multiplied to feed five-thousand men, along with the women and children who accompanied them. This is an impressive miracle by any standards, but it does not end there, because the disciples collect twelve baskets of leftovers. This detail points to a level of abundance that is hard to fathom. The fact that this miracle is recounted in every gospel points to the uniformity of God's abundance that is associated with Jesus' message and ministry.

Jesus' Ministry

When Jesus preached by the Sea of Galilee, multitudes gathered to hear the message of wisdom and hope. Hundreds of attendees at such an occasion would be impressive, but the New Testament speaks of multitudes. Crowds hem Jesus into houses as he starts to heal people. They pursue Jesus so tenaciously he has to get into waiting boats. When Jesus compares God's kingdom to a mustard seed (Luke 17:6)—the seed that produces a bush so tenacious that ancient farmers found it difficult to contain—he describes a force that could provoke an overwhelmingly abundant yield. The stories illustrate God's abundant offering to humankind.

Summary

This thematic exploration of biblical topics is by no means exhaustive, but merely suggestive of the types of themes that span the Old and New Testaments. In addition to the ones I have mentioned, it would be easy to find passages to illustrate preaching themes on perseverance, suffering, hope, justice, stewardship, healing, peace, forgiveness, vocation, temptation, and other similar themes that the Bible explores at length through stories, poetry, and prose.

What makes this exercise of identifying biblical themes so rich for the preacher is the fact that the waters of faith found in scripture are not shallow pools of simplistic understanding. These stories reward our curiosity with new insights, and reveal deep rivers of meaning with each new reading. In Genesis, when God creates humans from the dust of the earth, the image is one of a potter on a riverbank. As we come again and again to dip our feet into these sacred waters, we gain a clearer sense of the One who kneels, working with that mud quietly, and persistently, along the shoreline of life's profound truths.

These biblical themes describe a covenant relationship between the people and God that spans almost forty centuries. Jesus of Nazareth became the embodiment of that covenant, and illustrates many aspects of it. The Bible stories in the New Testament continue the thematic groundwork that has been laid in the Old Testament. Tracing these themes through the Bible stories, in both testaments, offers resources for this new paradigm for planning worship.

6

Launching a New Preaching Model

INTRODUCING THEMATIC PREACHING

CHANGE CAN BE HARD, but it does not have to be hard. A strategic approach to introducing change in worship can make all the difference. I introduced the idea of sermon themes slowly over several years' time, but I did not talk about it very much. Though I had many questions about the lectionary myself, I did not seek to make an issue of the lectionary. Instead, I decided to give my people a taste of change even before anyone called it change. I began by offering sermon series as a special feature during high liturgical seasons like Lent and Advent.

Lent

The notion of a Lenten sermon series was not innovative. Pastors have been preaching such series for decades to distinguish Lent from the rest of the year, and heighten its spiritual impact. I started with a set of sermons on the Lord's Prayer, and preached each week on a different line of the prayer. Another year during Lent, I preached a series on the seven deadly sins, updating a concept from the second century CE and explaining the contemporary relevance of each of these sins.[1] A series on sin turned out to be a much anticipated event.

Another Lenten theme was entitled, "Questions of Faith: A Primer on Faith Practices." Each sermon in that series took on a common question of faith today and tried to answer it. We addressed things like, How do I pray?, Where do I find hope?, How do I forgive?, and, Why do bad things happen to good people? The format of this series allowed me to share theological information, biblical resources, and practical psychological advice. I was surprised to see how many people were more curious about these topics when I presented them in a sustained, consistent fashion, instead of a sermon here or there. Something about the momentum that built week after week re-enforced the impact of each sermon. Before the series started, I solicited questions from the congregation to discover what they wanted to hear about, and gauged whether my first list of ideas would work. By asking people for their questions, I could tailor the series specifically to real concerns instead of imagined ones. Asking for feedback helped to reach not only those who are usually vocal about requests, but helped me reach a larger group of people who were curious, but hesitant, to ask for anything. Originally I had created this series to offer instruction to our newer members, but I discovered this sermon series found a welcome audience among the seasoned crowd, too.

One year, I took a leaf from Rick Warren's book and it worked even better than expected. To reach his audience, Warren studied learning styles and discovered that some people learn by hearing, others by seeing, and still others by actively doing something. In educational circles these learning patterns are called auditory, visual, and kinesthetic. Warren designed ways to reinforce his sermons on all of these teaching levels. Critical of preachers who

1. For this topic some preachers may need to preach on less than seven sins to make it all work out because Lent has only six weeks and one of them is Easter. However there are often extra opportunities to preach or write some devotionals during Holy Week, so preachers may be able to address any of the seven sins that did not fit into the series as it was presented in prime time.

limit their impact solely to oratory, which stimulates only auditory learning, he was among the pioneers in using large screens
effectively to present visual sermon outlines. In addition, Warren
provided paper in the service bulletins so the audience could take
notes and fill in a worksheet while he preached, enabling them to
hear, see, and write the message down.

One Lent, I developed a worksheet with a similar sermon
outline, so that the audience could take notes. It was such a new
idea that I expected only a handful of the congregation would want
a worksheet, and so I made enough copies for half the congregation. To my surprise, when these sheets ran out, some of the most
traditional members of the church—people who would have been
outraged if they had known the origin of this idea—were anxious
to get their own copies. We sent ushers to make more worksheets
in a hurry. What I learned that day was that people want to learn,
and these techniques are not tied to any ideology. (It probably did
not hurt that the myth of scarcity had suddenly made these worksheets seem increasingly valuable to people who thought that they
were being left out.)

Advent

In the third chapter I explained some of the ways that the lectionary readings in Advent run at odds with people's expectations when
they come to services in one of the most festive times in the Christian year. Two weeks focused on John the Baptist may prove a hard
pill to swallow. So, one of my first priorities was to try a different
approach to Advent. One Advent sermon series took its cues from
the candles on the Advent wreath, with sermons on hope, peace,
love, and joy. The next year, I created a series of sermons based on
characters in the Christmas story. These character studies offered
a variety of perspectives, and several years' worth of sermons.
Choices include, Joseph, Mary Elizabeth, Zechariah, Simeon, and
Anna. In each case, it is not hard to tell the story of the birth of
Jesus from the perspective of one of these characters. Though I
think it is hard to use John the Baptist for two of the four Sundays,

one sermon on John can offer a prophetic lens on the story of the incarnation. John's zeal sets the stage for a heightened expectation that can alert worshippers to the fact that Jesus is so much more than most of us can imagine. It is a question of balance, and while I believe it is wrong to have John dominate Advent, I also believe he has a place in the season. What I have done in Advent is downplay the theological notion that Advent anticipates the Second Coming of Christ. Moving away from the *New Revised Common Lectionary* made that possible.

Summer

One of the easiest times to preach a sermon series is during the summer. If you continue to use the lectionary and simply follow the Old Testament selections in Ordinary Time on the Christian calendar (which falls in the summertime in the northern hemisphere), the lectionary recounts the epic tales that lend themselves to the sermon series. While we were still very much in the experimental phase of this program, during the summer months we turned to the Old Testament readings to enjoy some of the epic tales of Judaism through texts that often seemed to preach themselves. To my surprise, a number of people said that they had never heard Bible stories explained like this before. I doubt that the stories had been overlooked before this, but I do believe the story telling made more sense when we took this same approach every week for the entire summer. Somehow it reinforced the messages in ways people could grasp, and gave them an opportunity to hear some of the best storytelling in the Bible. Week after week we looked at the journeys of Abraham, Isaac, and Jacob in cycle A, or the escapades of King David in cycle B, or the adventures of Elijah and Elisha in Cycle C. These dramas, with their character studies and life lessons, became a summer staple and laid the groundwork for the full transition to preaching with themes year round. Even preachers committed to continuing lectionary preaching might enjoy this option for a summer sermon series that makes Ordinary

Time anything but. This was such a positive experience that it laid the groundwork for more changes,

It was not until I went to Mars Hill, Rob Bell's church in Grand Rapids in June 2009, that I decided it was time for a complete worship overhaul. Something about the energy in that service, and the way that people responded to the sermon, convinced me we needed to make some major changes in our church services. Sitting through a sermon so much like the one I had preached two months before, and recognizing how much more effective Bell's sermon was when part of a series, convinced me we could not postpone this any longer. That fall I revised my sermon plans. So, I began this experiment in earnest and started preaching with themes every week.

I started with a series on Vocation.[2] When you start looking for examples of vocation, they are all over the Bible. The Bible is full of stories about people who were called by God. In the Old Testament, there is Abraham, Moses, Samuel, Esther, and Jeremiah. In the New Testament, there are great stories about the calls of Peter, Paul, Mary, Joseph, Mary Magdalene, and Zacchaeus. In the first series on Vocation, I used these examples to analyze and explore the nature of God's call in all of our lives. Comparing and contrasting the variety of ways that people experience God's transforming summons, I explained that the stories offer encouragement for all people who seek to find a new sense of purpose and direction.

The response to this set of sermons was quite dramatic. Attendance took a jump, and people started arriving with a new level of enthusiasm. They reported that they were learning more, and seeing things they never had seen before. One church leader told me, "You know I didn't want to admit this, but I never got much out of the Bible readings before. These topics make sense." A deacon remarked, "I love coming to church now on the first Sunday of the month, because you launch a whole new topic." Another congregant wrote one Saturday morning, "Susan, I find myself

---

2. At first, preaching about vocation reminded me of a Roman Catholic search for the novitiate, but the Bible is full of stories about God's call, and we took that tack.

wishing that the months were longer than they are, just so I can hear more sermons on each topic! Too bad tomorrow is the last Sunday in February. I never thought I'd wish for February to last longer!"

I used a survey to get some feedback, and sixty percent of our worshippers responded. Most of the feedback demonstrated widespread support for using monthly themes and for spending four to five weeks exploring a topic. Active members remarked that the themes had brought worship to life for them in new ways. One woman, a former chair of deacons, confessed to me that she felt she was beginning to understand the Bible for the first time because of this thematic approach. It was revealing to discover how much more people thought they got out of the services once we introduced the themes. It was also striking to see what a significant difference this *single* change produced.

When I began to choose themes for worship, I used several resources for the selection process. I gathered suggestions from church leaders, from the congregation, and from churches where theme preaching already had a successful tenure. Granted, this process of selecting themes had a certain quality of trial and error, but over time I began to recognize good themes for preaching more quickly. After experimenting for four years, I made a composite of a three-year cycle of our best themes, and those are the themes proposed in Appendix A. Each year's list is designed to include a balance of pastoral and prophetic topics, as well as a mix of meaty theological topics, themes that call for lessons from history, and themes that point toward contemporary issues. I believe this variety is essential each year so that while sermon series take advantage of their pedagogical potential, they don't seem like a faith syllabus, and the lessons are served up more subtly. Aware that the worshipping community includes people in different seasons of life, and coming with various questions of faith, I believe the sermons need to have a broad appeal each week and from month to month.

At the end of chapter 4, I introduced the Pulpit Curriculum with its list of sermon texts that I hope to address in sermons every three years. Because I feel so seriously about the teaching potential in preaching, I have set a pretty ambitious three-year list. But I recognize that passages which do not get pulpit air time can easily be addressed in other forums that supplement and support pulpit learning, like Bible study groups, and lectures. Hopefully, these themes have some currency over several sets of cycles, but, if we decide to amend the list of topics, the Pulpit Curriculum can serve as an ample source of texts.

For those who have been preaching from the lectionary for a number of years, changing to themed preaching is not a casual shift or quick adjustment. It may take time to orient to this new system. I realize that even with a set of preaching themes for a three-year cycle, and a list of good Bible stories, it can require a certain amount of work to find sermon texts for each theme, so in Appendix B I have created a list of suggestions for preaching on every theme. Appendix B offers at least five texts for each of the twenty-seven themes in the three-year cycle. Appendix B may prove to be the most helpful section in the whole book for those who decide to try this approach. It puts the whole system together in one place. Any preacher might create a different Pulpit Curriculum, or take the themes in the three-year cycle (Appendix A), and then survey the Pulpit Curriculum to choose other sermon texts, but Appendix B demonstrates one way to coordinate the three-year cycle, and the curriculum, in hopes of designing a bridge for those eager to experiment right away with preaching themes.

Paradigm Shift

As I reflect on my own journey from lectionary preaching to theme preaching, I cannot help but acknowledge how much energy it took to de-construct what I had been doing, and re-invent my own approach to worship. I want to find ways to make that process easier. Appendix A may help preachers imagine some alternatives much more quickly and easily. The three-year cycle of themes is designed for a nine-month program year, with one theme for each month. Decisions about the length of the year and how to organize the topics will vary from church to church. Some of these decisions will be more pragmatic than theological, if your church is anything like mine. In our church, summer worship is less formal and it offers the opportunity to address topics that do not fall naturally into the program calendar. It is a time to experiment or vet new ideas.

Appendix A includes a list of topics designed for the flow of congregational life in suburban churches, with which I am most familiar. Let me explain some of the thinking behind this pattern. Our program year begins in September, when Sunday school commences. September is the month when we have our largest crowd of newcomers. Fall themes are chosen for their broad appeal to people coming back to worship after a summer hiatus, and those who have never attended services at all.

Our attendance increases through the fall, until the largest audience appears between Advent and Easter. Therefore, I have chosen the most significant theological topics for February, March, and April. By this time in the program year, the newcomers have grown accustomed to the church, and can focus more on the pulpit message. They have established a routine with their children and any classrooms issues have been resolved.

The Pulpit Curriculum (Appendix C) offers a list of scripture readings that are central to our faith, and it is intentionally weighted toward stories rather than poetry, psalms, wisdom, or even prophetic literature. I find that storytelling offers texts that are easier to preach and teach about. In my critique of the *New Revised Common Lectionary,* I was quick to identify the prejudices of the consultation on common texts, with regard to the Hebrew Bible. I realize this Pulpit Curriculum is not without its own bias, or blind spots, but I have tried to use the Old Testament in a way that allows the faith lessons there to stand independently as resources for Christian worship. I believe that these ancient stories from the Hebrew Bible have stood the test of time for a reason, and I have tried to honor their original Jewish perspective.

Some of the biggest advocates for lectionary preaching caution that it is a good discipline for preachers to adhere to a set of assigned texts. Without the lectionary, they argue, preachers will be tempted, consciously or unconsciously, to choose sermon topics that are similar from week to week. The *New Revised Common Lectionary* forces them to address texts they do not like, and would never choose otherwise. In this way, lectionary preaching expands one's repertoire of sermons, and encourages preachers to delve into other parts of the Bible. While I appreciate this concern, I am not ultimately persuaded by it. In my experience, what makes a sermon fresh has nothing at all to do with the text that the preacher has chosen. Original scholarship or creative thinking may have no relation to the text at all. Many preachers deliver breathtaking sermons on a passage they have addressed repeatedly, but this time something makes the message thrilling. Other ministers preach virtually the same message every week, no matter what scripture lesson they read before they start to preach.

Everyone hopes a minister will stretch theologically, seek new resources, and find fresh interpretations of scripture. However, in my own experience, there have been times of rich new discovery, and other times of plodding and pedantic sermons. Some weeks afforded little time for study; on other weeks, some pastoral need unlocked my soul and I could preach on the dullest text and make it come alive. But some of my most effective sermons have been preached on texts that were very familiar, when I happened to gain some new insight that made my words sing a fresh tune. Whatever path a preacher takes, the level of freshness in sermons does not depend on who chooses the texts, the preacher, or the author of the lectionary. Some ministers, who pray each week and wait for the Lord to lay a text on their hearts, can produce sermons that are soaring masterworks of inspiration. By the same token, other preachers, who would never leave the lectionary for even one Sunday, may become known for their dry and predictable homilies. Most preachers have had moments when they found their soul unlocked by a text that came from the lectionary, and marveled at the ways that it seemed so pertinent to the issues in the church or the world. Conversely, the same preacher may strive to share some brand new ideas, but the only way to do that is to leave the lectionary and find a passage that illustrates his or her thinking.

The choice of the text is not what determines fresh preaching, but the way that the preacher connects personally to a scripture lesson. That can happen with or without the lectionary.

Sermon Preparation

One of the benefits of using themes for sermons is that it forces a preacher to prepare ahead of time. There is something about doing one topic for a whole series of sermons that makes sermon preparation easier and more efficient. Work on the first sermon in the series inevitably benefits the sermons that follow. As all the sermons in the series will be linked, material that does not fit in one can be used later in another. When theme preaching is taught in seminaries, professors suggest that students create folders for all the topics chosen for the year. This system sets up a ready file of stories and illustrations that pertain to the topics. With some discipline, preachers can collect ideas for each sermon theme or topic well ahead of time.

Once the series is organized, most preachers will continue to think about the topics, giving them conscious attention some days or simply mulling them over on other days. The benefit of this system is that it makes it more likely that sermons will be polished and thoughtful. Like the stock of a good stew that simmers on a back burner for a while, when it comes time to write the preacher begins with a mix of ideas that have been flavored with layers of thought. Sermons that carry the weight of several weeks, or even months, of reflection, are more likely to be substantive. It is hard to achieve that in one week's time, even with great diligence.

Selection of Themes and Preaching Topics

When I spoke to congregational leaders who have been successful using themed preaching, I realized that part of their success was the ability to solicit input, and run effective evaluations, without compromising the authority of the pulpit. The other lesson I learned was that effective themes are broad enough to allow for pastoral and prophetic messages. A good set of topics fits into the calendar, supports the annual teaching goals, and considers the needs of the congregation.

I recommend that clergy use a retreat for worship leaders to introduce theme preaching, and then a second retreat to evaluate it. Even one-day, off-site meetings offer an ideal space to consider the themes of the current year, and brainstorm some possibilities for the future. It was a big help to us to begin with ample time to plan, ruminate, discuss, and revise the ideas. Six months lead-time is not very long. First, as I mentioned, preachers can be more effective if they have time to organize and collect ideas for sermons; second, being organized eliminates the temptation for church members to make suggestions they expect to be incorporated right away. The lectionary provides its own order to worship. Those who try a new way to organize worship will have to find other methods of maintaining some of that sense of order. Advanced planning supports that stability.

Re-Enforcing the Theme

Theme preaching works best when you tell people the theme over and over. You cannot reinforce the theme too often. One reason for choosing themed preaching is because modern churches are full of people who are distracted with the many choices of modern life, but themes do not work any better than the lectionary unless they are emphasized. We put the theme on the cover of the service bulletin. I start every sermon telling people what the monthly theme is and why we chose it. In the newsletter, we ask all program staff to write about the theme. Bulletin boards illustrate the theme. When we first started preaching with themes, we used dramatic storytelling to illustrate the scripture lessons. You can use anything you want to support the theme: puppets, storytellers, film clips, special music, and art. Ideally, the themes could be addressed in weekly blogs, and seasonal devotions. There is no downside in searching for ways to repeat the themes in all appropriate church communications.

A new theme is launched on the first Sunday of each month, and while there is always a certain sense of suspense and added energy for the launch, we have not always been creative about introducing new topics. Since All Souls UU in Tulsa began the themed preaching approach, it has been adopted by UU churches in Minneapolis, Minnesota; Cleveland, Ohio; Washington DC., Bethesda, Maryland; and San Diego, California. In most of these congregations, the themes have been introduced each month with drama or special music on the first Sunday. Many churches choose a special story to introduce the topic to children and adults. In a conversation with Nancy McDonald Ladd, Senior Minister at River Road UU in Bethesda, MD, she was enthusiastic about the prominent place of the themes in the life of her congregation, and especially the first Sundays of each month, when the themes are introduced with special storytelling and music.

> Among the 12 most highly-attended Sundays in worship during 2013, ten of them coincided with the monthly first-Sunday rollout of our themes. It's like opening a present at the beginning of each month. People are eager to begin their own exploration of the theme and turn out to see the teaching story we're telling to illustrate it, share special music and gather for "going deeper" facilitated theme-based conversations after each service.[3]

Calendar Considerations

A key part of a smooth transition for those who start to preach with themes involves paying attention to the Christian calendar. Whether or not one uses the lectionary, it is essential to respect the Christian calendar. Themes chosen for Advent need to be appropriate for the weeks leading up to Christmas, and themes for the weeks of Lent also need to fit the feel of that season of pious

---

3. Ladd, interview.

reflection. Sermon themes will not work if they compete with the calendar, or run at cross-purposes with major holidays. It is also important to coordinate the sermon themes with important secular observances. Speaking about racism in January allows for a big emphasis on Martin Luther King Jr.'s birthday. Focusing on gratitude in November effectively addresses a topic that is already in people's minds as they prepare for Thanksgiving. Planning a series on love, to coincide with Valentine's Day, might be a way to offer a religious view of this largely secular holiday.

The date for Easter can fall between March 23 and April 24, so the themes for those two months have to take this major event into account. If the theme is broad enough, and chosen carefully, it can accommodate Easter. Otherwise, it might make more sense to treat Easter as a separate day, and depart from the monthly theme entirely. For us, the challenge has been to look at scripture in a broad and comprehensive way when choosing themes. Some of the most interesting themes for preaching are obvious when you step back and consider the stories of the Bible with a panoramic perspective.

One year, as I thought about how many of Jesus' disciples ran from the tomb because they were too stunned to take it in, it occurred to me that Easter was a colossal surprise to everyone close to Jesus, and that most of us forget that fact. As I reflected on the Bible stories, I realized that a great majority of the plot lines hinged on one surprise from God after another. So, I chose the theme of "surprise" for April. I found so many Bible stories with the theme of surprise that it was hard to limit the topic to one month. Then, on Easter, I talked about the resurrection as part of a long line of God's surprises for us. As part of the Easter sermon, I reviewed a list of Bible stories that stunned people, and I asked the congregation to yell "surprise" together at the end of each illustration. It ended up being fun for everyone, and a true surprise in word and deed. After several years of experimenting with the Easter season, I discovered that often, with a little creativity, the themes can give the Easter message a new currency.

Preacher's Prerogatives and Instincts

Some of the best themes are simple and intuitive. "Neighbor" proved to be one theme that everyone seemed to understand immediately. The topic offered a natural link to the story of the good Samaritan, which Jesus told in answer to the question, "But who is my neighbor?" (Luke 10:25). The theme also gave me a chance to preach about how we treat strangers, what appropriate boundaries look like, the justice concerns in immigration questions, and the responsibility of being a neighbor in a multicultural world.[4]

Some of the most creative ideas for themes came from suggestions that I got shaking hands at the door after worship. Not everything worked, but many ideas turned out to be real gems that I would not have thought of on my own. But, ultimately, every minister has to trust his or her own instincts about what *will preach*. The preacher is the one who will have to wrestle with a concept, find good texts, and do the exegetical work to make these themes come to life. No matter how popular the topic, no one will enjoy the sermon series if the preacher cannot speak effectively about it.

Pastors also need to be sure that the themes speak to the congregation's true needs, and don't restrict that kind of communication. This became most clear when I was preaching during Advent one year and my theme was "incarnation." The church was fuller than usual, as it was just a few days after a gunman had broken into Sandy Hook Elementary School in Newtown, Connecticut, and fatally shot twenty kindergarten students and six teachers there in 2012. As I preached about my assigned topic, I could feel the tension, and a certain air of mild distraction, in the sanctuary. That tension did not dissipate until I departed from my prepared remarks and took some time to talk about the shooting and address the sorrow, the fear of parents, and the shock and disillusionment of all of our parishioners. Once I did that, the congregation breathed an audible sigh of relief, because we were finally

---

4. For this series, we suggested that the church read a book about being a good neighbor. *My Neighbor's Faith: Stories of Interreligious Encounter, Growth and Transformation* by Jennifer Howe Peace, Or N. Rose and Gregory Mobley, editors. Maryknoll, New York: Orbis Books, 2012.

addressing the elephant in the room. Knowing what I know now, I would have abandoned my announced remarks, and the monthly topic entirely, to talk more specifically about this tragedy that had touched so many in my church.

Not long after that, the chair of deacons talked to me. His comment was very supportive, as he urged me to preach from my heart, weighing current events, and my conscience, while respecting the themes as a guide for the sermons each month. This philosophy allows for the freedom to let go of the theme when something really important happens in the news, or simply stirs our souls. Without this freedom, this program becomes a straitjacket, and I believe this method of preaching will only wear well over time, if it is comes with a looser fit.

Room for Improvement

Since this whole project was an experiment, we learned from our mistakes, and we made plenty along the way. But we began the project with a sense of freedom and gave ourselves permission to take some chances and enjoy the steep learning curve that trial and error offer. So, when we recognized something was amiss, we did a course correction and never looked back. When we stumbled into a successful plan, we took courage and kept going. Here are some places where we could make this program better.

Coordinating Pulpit Curriculum and Christian Education

We could do a better job of coordinating the curriculum for children, and youth, so that it connects with the preaching themes. With better planning, we could coordinate the lessons in worship and classrooms so we leverage this pedagogical opportunity. There is the potential here to create a church-wide curriculum, which is keyed into the Pulpit Curriculum, with teaching goals for various levels of learning. The hope would then be that we can reach our audience more effectively, and increase the teaching potential in this approach to worship. Families might leave the church having heard similar stories and lessons presented in different forums and ways. With more concerted effort in this area, the church could better coordinate its messages, so family conversations at home re-inforce Sunday's lessons all week long. One key component of this approach would be a programmatic approach that reoriented all the adult education offerings to be more thematic. I might include lectures, Bible study, and small group discussions on the monthly theme. Increasingly, I have come to see that church members are continually bombarded with messages from a variety of savvy sources. If the church's messages have any hope of penetrating this screen of information, then we will at the very least need to learn how to be more consistent and focused in our approach to what we convey and how we convey it.

Congregational Input

The best preaching opens the way to a conversation throughout the congregation. People appreciate opportunities to respond to sermons. Some churches provide space outside the sanctuary where people can post responses to the sermon theme, and each month worshippers responded to the sermons with notes, poems, photographs, drawings, and other handmade artwork. It provides a chance for the congregation to weigh in on the theme and re-flect on how the sermons made an impact on them. Formal and informal feedback improves a preacher's antennae for the religious questions that people are asking. Even negative feedback helps the preacher to assess what people gleaned from the sermons they have heard.

In the end, regardless of the feedback, a minister must assume responsibility for the themes that are finally chosen, because he or she will have to produce sermons on these themes in a way that invites the congregation to step onto holy ground. The freedom of the pulpit is a right that people fought for in the Protestant Ref-ormation. Some clergy paid the ultimate price so that preachers today might have the privilege of speaking the Word of God each week in the way they believe they are led to do. That calling challenges pastors to remember that, while they need to be sensitive to the questions of the flock, they are mostly responsible for stepping up to the task of being the shepherd of their souls.

Conclusion

Each week in churches across the country, pastors step into the pulpit to speak about life and faith. We strive to share wisdom that will bring people new perspective and hope for their lives, and the life of the world. I imagine that I am not the only one who sees something in the eyes of the people that raises the stakes on this enterprise. There is always the possibility for a very solemn trust to emerge in those moments when the earth may seem to stand still and something sacred hangs in the air, if only for a moment. That possibility that we might slip off our sandals and stand before God keeps preachers striving to listen more accurately, to teach more often, to study the Bible more earnestly, and to see new ways to tell the stories of faith.

In chapter 1 I traced the history of change in worship patterns. I mentioned that the *New Revised Common Lectionary* was introduced to most mainline Protestant churches in the middle of the twentieth century as an outgrowth of the ecumenical movement that followed two world wars. It was one component of a vision of a new era in Christian unity. The hope was that all Christian churches would be reading from the same scripture lesson every week, and that studying God's word in parallel worship services would have a unifying impact. For many years it accomplished that purpose. In fact, in recent decades, mainline Protestants who have built closer relationships, if not open communion, make assumptions today about ecumenism that were unthinkable, even in the middle of the twentieth century. No doubt the *New Revised Common Lectionary* has contributed to this ecumenical progress. But this approach to Christian unity emerged in an era of strong institutional loyalty; that feeling of loyalty made sense in the decades after World War II, but no longer makes sense for many people today.

The very reason the lectionary was developed may not be as relevant to churches today. Statistics show that fewer and fewer people in churches have the denominational loyalty that they had even fifty years ago. When Americans search for a church home, research demonstrates that many people no longer choose a church because they identify as a Lutheran, Methodist, or Episcopal. Their choices are affected more often by the size of the youth programs, the socio-economic feel of the church, the pastor's preaching style, and the architecture of the building.[5] Today, Protestant churches include many members who come from other denominations where worship may have been very different.

Ecumenism may not be the issue for churches today. We may have achieved so much on that front that it is time to declare victory and look more closely at some of the other challenges that face the church today. Unfortunately, by staying focused on the ecumenical goal, we may not recognize that we are in danger of losing a much more important challenge—the challenge to make our churches relevant to a wider audience, with their growing expectation that all aspects of life should be intuitive, including worship. Questioning the use of the *New Revised Common Lectionary* is one way to address this call for more intuitive worship patterns. While I am not alone among pastors and theologians who are raising questions about it, I have proposed a new approach to worship that has some far-reaching implications.

Though we remain committed to preaching with themes, in many ways it is still in the experimental stages, and we learn a lot every year. I won't try to prove that preaching with themes is always more effective than using the *New Revised Common Lectionary*. Real research on this transition is beyond the scope of this book. But I will be content with an abundance of anecdotal evidence that this new approach is reasonably successful for us, right now. The topics we have chosen, and that I suggest in Appendix A, are not definitive as much as suggestive, and I assume that any church or

5. Sellers, "Brand Loyalty," 3–5.

preacher might develop their own list of preaching themes and texts. Every bit as important as the list of Preaching Themes (contained in Appendix A), is the Pulpit Curriculum (contained in Appendix C). My hunch is that most ministers have their own pulpit curriculum in mind, but the exercise of being explicit about it may help to establish more effective sermons goals.

Over the years as I have continued to wonder about how best to share faith with modern worshipers. I have been overwhelmed and inspired in turns. My experience talking to young adults at that Boston coffee shop made a deep impression on me. It reminded me that the audience we are called to reach is much bigger than the people who happen to attend a service in our churches. I continue to ponder what it might mean to respond to that larger audience who may not attend worship very often, if ever, but who nonetheless ask probing religious questions and seek spiritual resources. When I think about that afternoon, I don't really worry so much about how to attract that young adult population to my church as about what the lesson in those conversations is for those of us who are leading established congregations. What those young adults represent in my mind is an earnest population, in the general public, with a deep spiritual hunger. For me, these folks represent all those people who might welcome a faith community, but who do not regard most established churches as reliable resources in their quest. It seems to be such a lost opportunity and yet such a hopeful realization at the same time.

When I become overwhelmed at this prospect, I find some comfort in the knowledge that throughout the history of our faith, times of great confusion often set the stage for new ideas and creative thinking. When the printing press was invented in the sixteenth century, the general populace was thrown into confusion at the sudden explosion of information. Historians have linked the technological explosion associated with the printing press to the subsequent Protestant Reformation. Perhaps today's technological explosion of information is creating a similar moment in time. As we adjust to the tidal wave of information, perhaps we may find there are also waves that carry us to new faith practices, if we can only figure out how to ride those waves.

Appendix A
Three Year Cycle of Themes

YEAR I

September	Hospitality
October	Vocation
November	Stewardship
December	Hope
January	Justice
February	God
March	Prayer
April	Surprise
May	Freedom

YEAR II

September	Neighbor
October	Covenant
November	Gratitude
December	Peace
January	Resilience
February	Jesus
March	Healing
April	Abundance
May	Reformation

YEAR III

September	Faith
October	Family
November	Forgiveness
December	Love
January	Good
February	Evil
March	Spiritual Journey
April	Resurrection
May	Creation

Appendix B
Coordinating Themes with Biblical Curriculum

HERE IS A LIST of sermon themes with suggestions for scripture lessons that make suitable preaching texts for each theme. I have endeavored to make several suggestions for every theme so that the preacher has some choices about how to approach these topics. As we have made the transition to themed preaching after using the lectionary for many years, it has become clear to me that the change in the way we organize worship has not been insubstantial, and this tool may be useful in offering suggestions and ideas for how to embark on such a new journey in pulpit discourse.

YEAR I

Hospitality

- Angels visit Abraham and Sarah (Gen 18:1–15)
- Rejection at Nazareth (Luke 4:14–30)
- Zacchaeus (Luke 19:1–10)
- Mary of Bethany (John 12:1–8)
- Jesus washes the feet of his disciples (John 13:1–20)
- Good Samaritan, Luke (10:25–37)
- Great Dinner (Matt 22:1–14; Luke 14:15–24)

Appendix B

Vocation

- Call of Abraham (Gen 15:1–6)
- Moses at the burning bush (Exod 3:1–12)
- Call of Samuel (1 Samuel 3:1–14)
- Call of Esther (Esther 4:9–14)
- Jesus calls the disciples (Matt 4:18–22; Mark 1:16–20; Luke 5:1–11)
- Conversion of Saul (Acts 9:1–13)

Stewardship

- Parable of the Talents (Matt 25:14–30)
- Feeding the 5000 (John 6:1–15)
- Riches (Matt 19:16–30; Mark 10:17–31; Luke 18:18–30)
- Parable of the Sower (Matt 13:1–23; Mark 4:1–9)
- Ananias and Saphira, (Acts 5:1–11)

Hope

- Zachariah's hope (Luke 1:5–23)
- Joseph's hope (Matt 1:18–25)
- Mary's hope (Luke 1:26–55)
- Creation (Gen 1)
- The resurrection (Mark 16:1–8; John 20:11–18)
- Lazarus (John 11:1–44)

Justice

- Nathan talks to King David (2 Samuel 12:1–15)
- Naboth's vineyard (1 Kgs 21)
- Laborers in the Vineyard (Matt 20:1–16)
- Parable of Lazarus and the Rich Man (Luke 16:19–31)

- Esther saves her people (Esther 4)

God

- Garden of Eden (Gen 3:1–13; 20–21)
- Good Shepherd (Psalm 23)
- The Lost Sheep (Luke 15:1–7)
- The Prodigal Son (Luke 15:11–32)
- God and Jesus (John 3:16–21)

Prayer

- Manna in wilderness (Exod 16:1–8)
- Advice on prayer (Matt 6:7–18)
- Gethsemane (Matt 26:36–46; Mark 14:32–42; Luke 22:40–46)
- Peter and the Holy Spirit (Acts 10:1–48)
- Job prays for friends (Job 42:1–9)

Surprise

- Anointing David (1 Samuel 16:6–13)
- The Ninevites repent (Jonah 3:6–10)
- Jesus and children (Mark 10:13–16)
- Wedding at Cana (John 2:1–12)
- Conversion of Saul (Acts 9:1–30)

Freedom

- Crossing the Red Sea (Exod 14:10–29)
- The Syrophoenician Woman (Matt 15:21–28; Mark 7:24–30; Luke 8:40–56)
- Healing the Paralytic (Mark 2:1–12; Matt 9:1–8; Luke 5:17–26)
- Philip baptizes an Ethiopian eunuch (Acts 8:26–40)

- Paul and Silas in jail (Acts 16:16–40)

YEAR II

Neighbor

- Good Samaritan (Luke 10:25–37)
- Lazarus and the Rich Man (Luke 16:19–31)
- Naboth's Vineyard (1 Kgs 21)
- Elisha and the Shunammite Woman (2 Kgs 4:8–10)
- Commandments on neighbors (Exod 20:16–17)
- Neighbors on the borders (Ruth 1:15–19)

Covenant

- The Ten Commandments Series No other gods (Exod 20:1–7)
- God's name and Sabbath (Exod 20:8–11)
- Honor your family (Exod 20:12, 14)
- Murder, adultery, stealing (Exod 20:13–15)
- Treating neighbors (Exod 20:16–17)
- God's covenant with Noah (Gen 8:20–9:17)
- Moses, Exod (34:1–10)
- The Last Supper (Matt 26:17–29)

Gratitude

- Feeding the 5000 (John 6:1–14)
- The Ten Lepers (Luke 17:11–19)
- Paul grateful in everything (1 Thes 5:12–18)
- Hebrews dance of thanksgiving (Exod 15:1–21)
- Riches (Matt 19:16–30, Mark 10:17–31, Luke 18:18–30)
- Samaritan woman (John 4:1–30)

Peace

- Stilling the storm (Matt 8:23–27, Mark 4:35–41, Luke 8:22–25)
- Washing feet (John 13:1–20)
- Beatitudes (Matt 5:1–12)
- Geresene demoniac (Matt 8:28–34, Mark 5:1–20, Luke 8:26–39)
- Lost sheep (Luke 15:1–7)
- Birth narrative (Luke 1:45–55) (Several sermons worth)

Resilience

- Jacob wrestling (Gen 32:22–32)
- Ruth leaves home (Ruth 1:1–4:22)
- Joseph (Gen 41:14–45)
- Moses (Exod 34:1–10)
- Job remains faithful (Job 42)

Jesus

- Nicodemus questions Jesus' identity (John 3:1–10)
- Light of the world (John 3:16–21)
- Humble healer (Matt 15:21–28, Mark 7:24–30 Mark 9:20–29)
- Storyteller–Parable of Sower (Matt 13:1–23, Mark 4:1–9)
- Subversive (Matt 5:38–42)

Healing

- Elijah heals a boy (1 Kgs 17:17–24)
- Man born blind (John 9:1–12)
- Woman with blood (Luke 8:43–56)
- Paralytic (Matt 9:1–8, Luke 5:17–26, Mark 2:1–12)
- Syrophoenician woman (Matt 15:21–28, Mark 7:24–30)
- Woman and daughter (Matt 9:18–26, Mark 5:21–43, Luke 8:40–56)

Abundance

- Creation (Gen 1)
- Laborers in the vineyard (Matt 20:1–16)
- Wedding at Cana (John 2:1–12)
- Feeding the 5000 (Matt 14:13–21, Mark 6:32–44, Luke 9:10–17, John 6:1–15)
- Mary of Bethany (John 12:1–8)
- Peter & Cornelius (Acts 10:1–48)

Reformation

- Reformed Ninevites (Jonah 3:1–4:5)
- Esther (Esther 1:1–10:3)
- John the Baptist (Matt 3:1–12, Mark 1:1–8. Luke 3:1–20)
- Conversion of Saul (Acts 9:1–30)
- Inclusion in church Ethiopian eunuch (Acts 8:26–40)
- Peter and Cornelius (Acts 10:1–48)

YEAR III

Faith

- Anointing David (1 Sam 16:1–13)
- Walking on water (Matt 14:22–33, Mark 6:45–52, John 6:16–21)
- Syrochoenician woman (Matt 15:21–28, Mark 7:24–30)
- Parable of Talents (Matt 25:14–30)
- In community (Numbers 11:4–18)
- Pentecost (Acts 2:1–13)
- Doubting Thomas (John 20:19–29)
- Conversion of Saul (Acts 9:1–30)
- Peter & Cornelius (Acts 10:1–48)

Family

- Bonds between generations (Ruth 1:6–19)
- Jacob & Esau (Gen 27:1–38)
- Kinship responsibilities (Ruth 3:1–13)
- Jesus in Temple (Luke 2:41–52)
- Jesus' family (Matt 12:46–50, Mark 3:31–35, Luke 8:19–21)
- Prodigal Son (Luke 15:11–32)
- Mary & Joseph (Matt 1:18–25)
- Elizabeth & Zechariah, aging well (Luke 1:5–25)

Forgiveness

- God's forgiveness Prodigal Son (Luke 15:11–20)
- Forgiving a sibling Prodigal Son Pt 2 (Luke 15:25–32)
- Unforgiving Servant (Matt 18:21–35)
- Forgiving God (Job 42:1–6)
- Forgiving others (Jonah 4)

Love

- God's love (Gen 1:26–31)
- Paul's chapter on love (I Corinthians 13)
- Jesus & children (Mark 10:13–16, Matt 19:13–15, Luke 18:15–17)
- John the Baptist—tough love (Luke 3:1–14)
- Limits of love (Matt 12:46–50, Mark 3:31–35, Luke 8:19–21)
- Ten Bridesmaids—tough love (Matt 25:1–13)

Good & Evil

- Cain and Abel (Gen 4:1–16)
- Jacob steals the birthright (Gen 27:1–40)

- Pride of Naaman (2 Kgs 5)
- David & Bathsheba (11 Samuel 11:1–27)
- Nathan talks to David (11 Samuel 12:1–15)
- Zacchaeus Luke (19:1–10)
- Judas (Matt 26:47–56, Luke 22:47–48)

Spiritual Journey

- Stages of Faith Series based on ExodCall at burning bush (Exod 3:1–12)
- Facing Pharaoh (Exod 4:18–20, 5:1-9 ff.)
- Crossing the sea (Exod 14:1–25)
- Manna in wilderness (Exod 16)
- Faith in community (Exod 19, 20)
- Promised Land (Deut 34, Joshua 5:13–6:16)
- Saul becomes Paul (Acts 9:1–30)
- Ethiopian eunuch (Acts 8:26–40)
- Road to Emmaus (Luke 24:13–32)

Resurrection

- Jesus (John 20:1–18, Luke 24:1–12, Mark 16:1–8, Matt 28:1–10)
- Elisha and Shunammite boy (2 Kgs 4:32–37)
- Lazarus (John 11:1–44)
- Road to Emmaus (Luke 24:13–32)
- Jesus appears to his disciples (Luke 24:36–49)
- Jesus on beach (John 21:1–14)

Creation

- Story of creation (Gen 1 and 2)
- Sermon on Mount (Matt 6:25–33)

- The Earth is the Lord's (Ps 24)
- Parable of the Sower (Matt 13:1–23, Mark 4:1–20, Luke 8:4–15)
- Spiritual gifts (1 Cor 12:1–31)

Appendix C
Pulpit Curriculum

HERE WE HAVE A list of suggested scripture readings that constitute a core pulpit curriculum. This list of scripture lessons offers a va¬riety of texts for sermons from both the Old and New Testaments. Themes for worship can be illustrated from the preaching texts available below. Within a three–year cycle, the congregation should be hearing a sermon that addresses each of these texts at least once every three years. So this list of scripture provides a core curriculum for the congregation, and a set of required passages for the preacher to address, rotating through the various options triennially. While this list is by no means exhaustive, it is a good guide to the more prominent passages at the center of the Christian faith. It can always be tweaked, amended, and supplemented, as the preacher deems necessary.

CORE SCRIPTURE CURRICULUM FOR PREACHING

Old Testament

Creation Stories	Gen 1:1–2:4, Gen 2:4–3:24
Cain and Abel	Gen 4:1–16
Noah	Gen 6:5–9:17

Tower of Babel   Gen 11:1–9

Abraham and Sarah

Visitors promise a son   Gen 18:1–15
Isaac born, Hagar sent away   Gen 21:1–21
Sacrifice of Isaac   Gen 22:1–19

Jacob

Jacob steals the birthright   Gen 27:1–38
Jacob wrestling with angel   Gen 32:22–32

Joseph

Joseph's coat and dreams   Gen 37:1–36
Joseph interprets Pharaoh's dreams   Gen 41:14–45

Moses

Burning bush   Exod 3:1–12
Facing Pharaoh   Exod 4:18–20, 5:1–9
Crossing the Red Sea   Exod 14:1–31
Manna in the wilderness   Exod 16
Ten Commandments   Exod 19–20
Promised Land   Deut 34, Josh 5:13–6:16

Ruth

Staying with Naomi   Ruth 1
Ruth and Boaz   Ruth 3:1–4:22

Samuel

Call of Samuel   1 Sam 3:1–14
Anointing David   1 Sam 16:1–13

David

David and Goliath   1 Sam 17:1–49
The Ark comes to Jerusalem   2 Sam 6:1–23
David and Bathsheba   2 Sam 11:1–27
Nathan's Parable   2 Sam 12:1–15

Elijah

Widow of Zarephath   1 Kgs 17:8–24
Triumph over Priests of Baal   1 Kgs 18:20–40

New Testament

Zacchaeus   Luke 19:1–10

Teachings

Beatitudes   Matt 5:1–12
Prayer   Matt 6:7–18
Riches   Matt 19:16–30, Mark 10:17–31, Luke 18:18–30

Disciples

Calling Disciples   Matt 4:18–22, Mark 1:16–20, Luke 5:1–11
Washing the feet   John 13:1–20

Miracles

Wedding at Cana   John 2:1–12
Stilling the Storm   Matt 8:23–27, Mark 4:35–41, Luke 8:22–25
Feeding 5000   Matt 14:13–21, Mark 6:32–44, Luke 9:10–17,
                                                         John 6:1–15
Walking on Water   Matt 14:22–33, Mark 6:45–52, John 6:16–21
Lazarus   John 11:1–44

Healings

Paralytic   Matt 9:1–8, Mark 2:1–12, Luke 5:17–26
Gerasene Demoniac   Matt 8:28–34, Mark 5:1–20, Luke 8:26–39
Woman & Girl   Matt 9:18–26, Mark 5:21–43, Luke 8:40–56
Syrophoenician Woman   Matt 15:21–28, Mark 7:24–30
Man Born Blind   John 9:1–34

Parables

Sower   Matt 13:1–23, Mark 4:1–20, Luke 8:4–15
Unforgiving Servant   Matt 18:23–35
Laborers in Vineyard   Matt 20:1–16
Bridesmaids   Matt 25:1–13
Talents   Matt 25:14–30
Good Samaritan   Luke 10:25–37
Great Dinner   Matt 22:1–14, Luke 14:15–24
Lost Sheep   Matt 18:12–14, Luke 15:1–7
Prodigal Son   Luke 15:11–32
Lazarus and the Rich Man   Luke 16:19–31

Passion Narrative

Entry into Jerusalem   Matt 21:1–11, Mark 11:1–11, Luke 19:28–38,
                                                        John 12:12–19

Last Supper	Matt 26:17–29, Mark 14:12–21, Luke 22:7–22, John 13:21–26
Garden of Gethsemane	Matt 26:36–46, Mark 14:32–42, Luke 22:40–46
Peter's Denial	Matt 26:31–35, 26:69–75; Mark 14:66–72, Luke 22:55–62, John 18:15-18, 25–27
Crucifixion death and burial	Matt 27:32–61, Mark 15:21–47, Luke 23:26–56, John 19:16–42

Resurrection

Empty tomb	Matt 28:1–8, Mark 16:1–6, Luke 24:1–12, John 20:1–18
Road to Emmaus	Luke 24:13–35
Thomas	John 20:19–29
Breakfast on the beach	John 21:1–14

Birth of the Church

Pentecost	Acts 2:1–13
Ethiopian Eunuch	Acts 8:26–40
Conversion of Saul to Paul	Acts 9:1–30
Peter & Cornelius	Acts 10:1–48

Teachings

Spiritual gifts	1 Cor 12:1–31
Love	1 Cor 13
Humility	Phil 2:1–11
Courage	Phil 3:12–16

Bibliography

Ackerman, David. *Beyond the Lectionary: A Year of Alternatives to the Revised Common Lectionary.* Winchester, UK: Circle Books, 2013.

The African American Lectionary: A Collaborative Project of the African American Pulpit and the American Baptist College of Nashville. http://theafricanamericanlectionary.org/

Arnett, Peter. *Emerging Adulthood: The Winding Road from Late Teens through the Twenties.* New York: Oxford University Press, 2004.

Bandy, Thomas G. *Introducing the Uncommon Lectionary: Opening the Bible to Seekers and Disciples.* Nashville: Abingdon, 2006.

Barna Group. "Barna Study of Religious Changes since 1991 Shows Significant Changes by Faith Group." https://www.barna.org/barna-update/faith-spirituality/514-barna-study-of-religious-change-since-1991-shows-significant-changes-by-faith-group#.VQHG-fnF-So.

Barnes, Rebecca and Lowry, Lindy 7 Startling Facts: An Up Close Look at Church Attendance in America. http://www.churchleaders.com/pastors/pastor-articles/139575-7-startling-facts-an-up-close-look-at-church-attendance-in-america.html.

Brooks, David. "How to Fight the Man." *The New York Times,* February 2, 2012. http://www.nytimes.com/2012/02/03/opinion/brooks-how-to-fight-the-man.html?_r=0.

Buckland, Patricia. *Advent to Pentecost: A History of the Christian Year.* Wilton, CT: Morehouse-Barlow, 1979.

Butcher, John Beverley. *An Uncommon Lectionary: A Companion to Common Lectionaries.* Santa Rosa, CA: Polebridge, 2002.

Calkins, Raymond. *The Christian Year and Its Practical Use in the Church Today.* New York: Commission on Evangelism and Devotional Life, 1936.

Chaliceworld: Solutions for Unitarian Universalist Lay-Led Ministry. "Monthly Themes at All Souls, Tulsa, Help Congregants Go Deeper." July 10, 2012. http://chaliceworld.com/2012/07/10/monthly-themes-at-all-souls-tulsa-help-congregants-go-deeper/.

Bibliography

The Consultation on Common Texts. *The New Revised Common Lectionary.* Nashville: Abingdon, 1992.

Copeland, Adam J. "No Need for Church: Ministry with Young Adults in Flux." *Christian Century,* February 8, 2012. http://www.readperiodicals. com/201202/2583768541.html.

Crossan, John Dominic. *God and Empire: Jesus Against Rome Then and Now.* New York: HarperCollins. 2007.

Gray Matter Research and Consulting. "Protestant Churchgoers are No More Loyal to their Brand of Denomination than they are to Brands of Toothpaste of Bathroom Tissue." 2009. http://www.greymatterresearch. com/index_files/Denominational_Loyalty.html.

Hoge, Dean R., et al."Influence of Role Preference and Role Clarity on Vocational Commitment of Protestant Ministers." *Oxford Journal of Sociology of Religion* 42 (1981) 1–16.

Jones, Jeffrey. *Traveling Together: A Guide for Disciple-Forming Congregations.* Herndon, VA: Alban Institute, 2006.

Kushner, Harold. *When Children Ask about God: A Guide for Parents Who Don't Always Have All the Answers.* New York: Schocken, 1989.

Levine, Amy-Jill. *The Misunderstood Jew: The Church and the Scandal of the Jewish Jesus.* New York: HarperOne, 2006.

Lipka, Michael. "What Surveys Say about Worship Attendance—and Why Some Stay Home." Pew Research Center, September 13, 2013. http://www. pewresearch.org/fact-tank/2013/09/13/what-surveys-say-about-worship-attendance-and-why-some-stay-home/.

Meyers, Robin. *Saving Jesus from the Church: How to Stop Worshipping Christ and Start Following Jesus.* New York: HarperOne, 2009.

Nardone, Richard M. *The Story of the Christian Year.* New York: Paulist, 1991.

Paulson, Michael. "Americans Claim to Attend Church More Than They Do" *New York Times,* May 17, 2014. http://nyti.ms/1lMzqVB.

Peace, Jennifer Howe, et al., eds. *My Neighbor's Faith: Stories of Interreligious Encounter, Growth and Transformation.* Maryknoll, NY: Orbis, 2012.

Pew Research Center: Religion and Public Life. "Nones on the Rise." October 9, 2012. http://www.pewforum.org/2012/10/09/nones-on-the-rise/.

Ring, Alexander. "The Path of Understanding: The Development of Lectionaries and Their Use in the Lutheran Church." Presented to the Evangelical Lutheran Synod General Pastoral Conference, Bloomington, MN, January 6, 1998.

Sellers, Ron. "Brand Loyalty in Church." *Clergy Journal,* May/June 2010, 3–5.

Slemmons, Timothy Matthew. *Year D: A Quadrennial Supplement to the Revised Common Lectionary.* Eugene, OR: Cascade Books, 2012.

Spong, John Shelby. *Jesus for the Non-Religious.* New York: HarperCollins, 2007.

Talley, Thomas. *The Origins of the Liturgical Year.* Collegeville, MN: Liturgical Press, 1986.

Telford, John. *The Life of John Wesley.* Wesley Center online. http://wesley.nnu. edu/?id=89.

Thorngate, Steven. "What's the Text? Alternatives to the Common Lectionary." *Christian Century,* 20–27, October 30, 2013.

Vest, John W. "Reflections on the Lectionary." *Christian Century,* February 19, 2014. http://www.readperiodicals.com/201402/3220476651.html.

Westerhoff, John H, III. *Will Our Children Have Faith?* New York: Morehouse, 2000.

Warren, Rick. *The Purpose Driven Church.* Grand Rapids: Zondervan, 1995.

Weiner, Eric. "Americans: Undecided About God?" *New York Times,* December 11, 2011. http://www.nytimes.com/2011/12/11/opinion/sunday/americans-and-god.html.

White, James F. *A Brief History of Christian Worship.* Nashville: Abingdon, 1993.